THE FABULOUS GIRLS' BOOK

Discover the Secret to Being FABULOUS

WRITTEN BY VEENA BHAIRO-SMITH

ILLUSTRATED BY NELLIE RYAN

THE FABULOUS GIRLS' BOOK

Discover the Secret to Being FABULOUS

PSS!
PRICE STERN SLOAN
An Imprint of Penguin Group (USA) Inc.

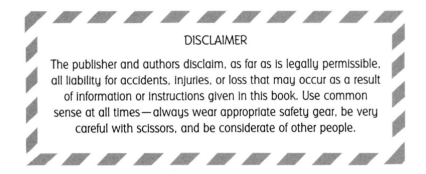

DISCLAIMER

The publisher and authors disclaim, as far as is legally permissible, all liability for accidents, injuries, or loss that may occur as a result of information or instructions given in this book. Use common sense at all times—always wear appropriate safety gear, be very careful with scissors, and be considerate of other people.

PRICE STERN SLOAN
Published by the Penguin Group
Penguin Group (USA) Inc., 375 Hudson Street, New York, New York 10014, USA
Penguin Group (Canada), 90 Eglinton Avenue East, Suite 700,
Toronto, Ontario M4P 2Y3, Canada
(a division of Pearson Penguin Canada Inc.)
Penguin Books Ltd., 80 Strand, London WC2R 0RL, England
Penguin Group Ireland, 25 St. Stephen's Green, Dublin 2, Ireland
(a division of Penguin Books Ltd.)
Penguin Group (Australia), 250 Camberwell Road, Camberwell, Victoria 3124, Australia
(a division of Pearson Australia Group Pty. Ltd.)
Penguin Books India Pvt. Ltd., 11 Community Centre,
Panchsheel Park, New Delhi—110 017, India
Penguin Group (NZ), 67 Apollo Drive, Rosedale, Auckland 0632, New Zealand
(a division of Pearson New Zealand Ltd.)
Penguin Books (South Africa) (Pty.) Ltd., 24 Sturdee Avenue,
Rosebank, Johannesburg 2196, South Africa

Penguin Books Ltd., Registered Offices: 80 Strand, London WC2R 0RL, England

ISBN 978-0-8431-9847-8   10 9 8 7 6 5 4 3 2 1

CONTENTS

NOTE TO THE READER

The publisher and authors disclaim, as far as is legally permissable, all liability for accidents, injuries, or loss that may occur as a result of information or instructions given in this book.

The most fabulous girls use their best common sense at all times. Be very careful with scissors, needles, kitchen equipment, and hot liquids, and get permission from the appropriate adult before using any tools or utensils. Stay within the law and local rules, and always be considerate of other people.

HOW TO APPEAR FABULOUSLY CONFIDENT

Some girls can cope with any situation—they appear calm and confident, smiling and chatting no matter what happens. However, that girl who is laughing and tossing her hair is probably secretly worried about the test everyone is taking tomorrow as well. You can look as cool as a cucumber, too, with these fabulous tips:

Prepare yourself: Run through the situation in your head beforehand and picture what could happen. Imagine responding in a positive way, so that when something similar happens you're ready. If you're taking a test, no preparation will do other than studying—so crack open the books ahead of time.

Embrace surprises: When something happens that you weren't expecting—and it probably will—just smile. Look at this surprise as an adventure rather than a shock, and enjoy it.

Believe in yourself: Tell yourself that you can do exactly what you need to in each situation you tackle and say the words out loud. This actually improves your confidence and increases your chances of doing really well.

Focus: Concentrate on what you're doing and give each situation 100 percent of your attention. Don't be distracted by other people's worries about what might happen later—keep your mind on what is happening NOW.

Fabulous tip: Give your confidence an extra boost with the shyness solutions on page 106—you're sure to be feeling fabulously confident in no time.

HOW TO BE FABULOUS
WITH MONEY

Wouldn't it be fabulous if you had enough money to buy everything you ever wanted? Unfortunately, that just isn't the case. The more money you have, the more you want, but follow these tips and you can make your money go further.

WATCH YOUR PENNIES

It's important to keep track of your money—how much you have and how much you're planning to spend. Here are some money-saving tips.

• It is much easier to save when you have a goal in mind. Make a list of all the things you want to buy and how much they cost. Then figure out how long it will take you to save your money for them.

• Be realistic. Cross off anything on the list that you don't really need or that you can make yourself. This way you will get your hands on the things you really want sooner.

• Every penny counts. Leave your wallet at home when you don't need it. Every magazine or hair clip you buy eats into your savings and leaves you further away from your prize.

GET YOUR HANDS DIRTY

Adults have to work to make a living and, even though going to school can sometimes be a chore, it isn't quite the same thing. You need to show your parents that you are prepared to work hard for extra money. Let them know what you are saving for and ask if there is anything you can do to help around the house or yard. Hopefully, they will admire your responsible attitude and reward your efforts with some extra cash.

MAKE DO AND MEND

Try jazzing up some old things you have. You will be surprised at how much you have lying around at home that can be transformed into something fabulous.

- Instead of buying a new outfit, use scarves, belts, or jewelry to update an old one (see page 111). Why not try pinning a homemade corsage onto an old coat for instant glamour (see page 101)?

- Making gifts for friends and family is a great way to save pennies—and handmade things are always extra special.

ONE GIRL'S TRASH IS ANOTHER GIRL'S TREASURE

You may be tired of some of your old things, but your friends might love them. Ask them to bring over all of their old CDs and accessories and hold a swap party. You can exchange things for a week or even for keeps. You will get yourself some really great new-to-you stuff without having to break open your piggy bank.

Warning: Don't forget to check with an adult before giving away any of your prized possessions.

HOW TO WIN A TALENT CONTEST

Winning a talent contest takes ambition, courage, and, of course, a talent that sets you apart from the other competitors. The key to winning often lies in impressing the audience rather than the judges. If the judges can see that the audience thinks you're fabulous, they are more likely to award you mega-points. Here's a handy guide to wowing the crowd.

TALENT TIPS

• You're probably a multitalented lady, but focus on one talent and stick with it. Someone juggling with fire while singing and baking cupcakes is less likely to impress than someone doing one thing really, really well.

• Whatever it is you're doing, you want the audience to enjoy it. Having a big grin on your face is a sure way to get them in the mood. Practice your facial expressions in front of a mirror, so that you look relaxed and happy, even if you're concentrating very hard.

• You want your performance to have the "wow" factor, so take time to prepare your look. You could wear something dazzling and sparkly, be lit by a single, blinding spotlight, or ask some friends to help by becoming your fabulous backup dancers.

HOW TO HOLD YOUR OWN AWARDS SHOW

Hollywood loves to hold awards shows and parties to celebrate the most talented actors and performers. Why not hold your own awards party to celebrate all the best qualities of your most fabulous friends?

AND THE NOMINEES ARE ...

Instead of invitations, you should send out nominations letting your guests know that they have been nominated for an award and where and when they can collect it.

Congratulations!

You have been nominated to receive the (insert name of the award category here) Award at the (insert name here) Awards.

Please come to (insert your address here) on (insert date here) at (insert time here) to receive your award.

Dress code: Red-carpet ready.

AWARD-WINNING FOOD AND DRINK

"Canapés" are a fabulous food for an awards party—think "finger food" that you can fit neatly into your mouth in one bite. You don't want to get food on your best clothes!

Finger sandwiches are perfect (see page 33) and miniature mozzarella balls or cubes of cheddar and cherry tomatoes on sticks really look the part. Mix Sprite or 7Up with orange juice for the perfect fizzy party drink.

DRESS THE ROOM

Awards shows always have a red carpet, and yours should be no different. Before your party, look out for any red fabric you can find—an old sheet or tablecloth is perfect, or even an old curtain from a thrift store. If you can't find any fabric, red paper will work just fine. Lay your carpet in the corner of your party room and at the party ask each of your guests to stand on the carpet in turn to have their photograph taken. Strike a pose!

Decorate the rest of the room with lots of gold balloons and sparkly streamers.

Make name cards to place on the seats so that your guests sit in the right chairs.

... AND THE WINNER IS ...

At this party, everyone is a winner of something! Throughout the party, stop the music to announce different awards for different categories. Use the list below to get you started.

☆ BEST DRESSED ☆
☆ FIRST TO ARRIVE ☆
☆ OLDEST FRIEND ☆
☆ NEWEST FRIEND ☆
☆ BEST SINGER ☆
☆ BEST MANNERS ☆
☆ BIGGEST DIVA ☆
☆ STYLE ICON ☆
☆ BEST AT DOING FUNNY VOICES ☆
☆ BEST AT SILLY WALKS ☆
☆ BEST DANCER ☆

THE PRIZE

The awards are your party favors. Fill party bags with little treats, such as a small bar of chocolate, a pretty eraser, a lip gloss, and a cute button or shell. When you give out each award, why not also present a sweet bouquet (see page 78) to each winner?

HOW TO SURVIVE EMBARRASSING MOMENTS

Whether it is calling your teacher "Mom" or tripping in front of your crush, embarrassing things happen to everyone from time to time. Follow the tips below to make sure you're ready to deal with even the most cringe-worthy situations with style.

DAMAGE CONTROL

After an embarrassing accident has happened, take a look around. Has anyone actually noticed? You may have been lucky and gotten away with it. People are often too busy thinking about how cool they are to notice your mistakes. If no one draws attention to your slipup, move on. There is no need to point it out yourself.

LAUGH IT OFF

If your mistake was too obvious for anyone to miss—such as falling over during a school play or tripping halfway down the catwalk—get up quickly and smile. People will love you for this. You may want the ground to open up and swallow you whole or to start a new life in another country, but the less embarrassed you show people you are, the less likely they are to tease you about it. If you appear not to be bothered, why should they be?

STAY COOL

Remain calm. This will help you avoid going red in the face. Develop the ability to brush off embarrassment. Getting upset will only draw more attention to yourself. Don't stick around and allow a crowd to gather around you. Leave the scene of your "crime against cool" with a good friend as soon as you can. You will soon be laughing about it.

PUTTING THINGS IN PERSPECTIVE

Cringe-worthy things happen to even the most fabulous of people. You may feel bad for a while and people may even tease you, but this will pass. Try not to get too upset over it. The more dramatic you are, the more you will remind people about what happened.

PRIDE COMES BEFORE A FALL

Try not to take yourself too seriously. If you strut around acting as if you are the best thing ever, don't be surprised if people find it particularly hilarious when you mess up. It is great to be confident, but being arrogant will make the most embarrassing moments much harder to deal with.

OTHER PEOPLE'S MISTAKES

Try to resist bursting out laughing or teasing someone when they slip up or have a mishap—however tempting it may be. Be a good friend and distract people's attention. Hopefully the next time the worst happens to you, they will be on hand to help you.

FIVE FABULOUS WAYS TO WEAR A SARONG

A sarong is every stylish girl's vacation essential. It doesn't cost much and takes up almost no space in your suitcase, but it is super useful.

THE SHORT SKIRT

This style is the perfect cover-up for an emergency ice-cream run.

Fold the sarong in half lengthwise. Then hold it behind your waist, with one of the top corners in each hand. Wrap it around your waist and secure it with a double knot at your hip.

THE LONG SKIRT

Here's a more sophisticated skirt for lunchtime at the beach café.

Place your sarong behind your waist, holding the two top corners out in front of you. Wrap the sarong around your middle by overlapping the corners you are holding. Pull the sarong tight and tuck the corners in tightly at the waist.

THE SUNDRESS

This fabulous frock is perfect for the beach and can double as a changing tent for getting in and out of your swimsuit.

Place the long edge of your sarong across the width of your back, just underneath your armpits. Hold both top corners out in front of you, then cross them over and tie them together behind your neck in a secure double knot.

THE BEACH BANDEAU

This is a lovely summery top and a fresh look with jeans or shorts.

Fold your sarong in half lengthwise and hold it over your chest and stomach. Pass the ends of the sarong under your arms, and secure it in place with a double knot at the back. Make sure the sarong is nice and tight to avoid any mishaps.

THE EVENING SHAWL

This style is a glamorous addition to any evening outfit, perfect for keeping the chill from your shoulders.

Fold the sarong in half lengthwise, and casually drape it around your shoulders.

HOW TO START YOUR OWN FASHION LABEL

Become a part of the fabulous world of fashion by starting your own designer label. This year your designs will be seen in your bedroom—next year they might be admired on the catwalk.

GET INSPIRED

Think about what type of collection you want to design. You could choose a glamorous range of evening wear or a young and funky collection of sportswear—it's up to you. Think about the kinds of clothes you most like to wear and what you would wear if you could buy anything you wanted.

When you have decided on your collection's theme, choose what type of "look" you want your clothes to have—frilly and feminine or modern and edgy—again, it's up to you.

Flip through all of your old magazines and cut out pictures of clothes, colors, or accessories that you particularly like. Glue these onto a sheet of paper and use them to help give you ideas while you are designing.

WHAT'S IN A NAME?

Every brand needs a name, and yours is no different. You could keep it simple and use your last name, or come up with a name that reflects the feel of your clothes such as "Jump!" for an exciting range of extreme sportswear or "Diva Divine" for a fabulous collection of ball gowns. Whatever name you choose,

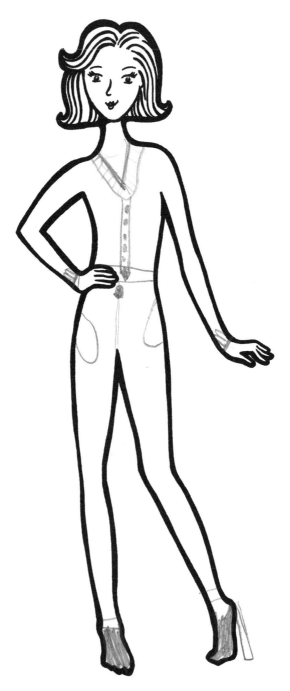

make sure you write it on the top right-hand corner of each of your designs along with the date to stop people from stealing your unique ideas.

GET CREATIVE

You will need:

a pile of fashion magazines • a sheet of thin cardstock • scissors • lots of plain paper • a pencil • colored pencils • a fabulous imagination

1. Take a sheet of plain paper and place it over the opposite page. Trace around the model using your pencil.

2. Glue your tracing onto a thin piece of cardstock and then cut it out. This will be your fashion template.

3. Take another sheet of plain paper and, using your pencil, draw around your template.

4. Now it is time to start designing. Draw on the basic shapes of your clothes first and then add details, such as buttons and bows.

5. When you have finished your design, color it in.

Fabulous tip: Designers keep their ideas in a book called a "portfolio." You can make your own very easily by punching holes in the left-hand side of your designs and binding them together with a ribbon following the instructions on page 73.

FABULOUS IS
AS FABULOUS DOES

If you have to tell people you are fabulous, you're not truly fabulous. Follow these steps to let your inner fabulousness shine.

FIVE RULES OF FABULOUSNESS

1. Always say "Please" and "Thank you" when you ask for things, and say it with a smile. People are much more willing to help you if they are asked politely.

2. When greeting people, offer your hand for them to shake. Grip their palm firmly and confidently. A weak handshake makes you look shy and unwilling to say "Hello."

3. Whether you are on a bus or in your own home, always offer your seat to an elderly person or someone who needs it more than you.

4. Try to look your best. This shows the people you meet that you respect them and that you take pride in the things you do.

5. Always remember, the more mean things you say, the more mean things will be said about you. Never say anything behind someone's back that you wouldn't say to their face.

HOW TO HAVE A FABULOUS CASCADE OF CURLS

Styling your hair into a cascade of curls couldn't be simpler and is guaranteed to give you a Hollywood-starlet look. Follow these simple steps with long hair for show-stopping style.

You will need:

an old sheet or large piece of fabric • a ruler • scissors • a hair elastic

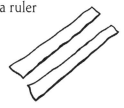

1. Cut your sheet or fabric into lots of strips, each measuring about 2 inches wide by 8 inches long.

2. Shampoo and condition your hair, then comb it while it is still damp until there are no tangles.

3. Separate your hair into two parts by twisting the top half of your hair into a looped topknot as shown. Secure this with a hair elastic.

4. Take a section of the hair that is still loose. It should be about an inch thick. Comb it again.

5. Take one of your fabric strips and fold it in half around the bottom of the section of hair as shown.

6. Roll the section of hair up the strip, so that the hair wraps around the width of the fabric. Try to wrap the hair around the strip tightly–the tighter you wrap, the bouncier your curls will be. Once you have reached your head, secure the strip by tying the two ends of the fabric in a knot.

7. Repeat this technique, rolling small sections of hair, until the bottom part of your hair is all in rolls.

8. Now let down the top part of your hair and comb it. Separate small sections of hair, each about an inch wide, and repeat steps **5** and **6** until the top part of your hair is all in rolls.

9. Let your hair dry. For best results leave it rolled up overnight. This might be a bit uncomfortable, but the results will be worth waiting for. If you really can't bear this, dry your hair with a hair dryer on its coolest setting.

LETTING YOUR HAIR DOWN

10. Once your hair has dried completely, it is time to remove your fabric strips. Undo the knot in each strip and carefully unravel your hair from it.

11. Continue to unravel all of the strips. Avoid running your fingers through the curls at this stage. They are much easier to manage while they are still tightly wound.

12. Put all of your fabric strips aside so you can use them again.

13. Style your hair by teasing the curls apart using your fingertips. If any of them are sticking out awkwardly, calm them down by spreading on a little water with the palms of your hands.

You should now have a head full of perfect curls. Gorgeous—and they will look even more fabulous tomorrow after you have slept on them for one night!

Fabulous tip: For super-glossy curls, spritz your hair with a leave-in conditioner while it is still damp and before you roll it in the strips.

HOW TO CREATE YOUR OWN COSTUME JEWELRY

Costume jewelry is a great way to make any outfit utterly fabulous. It lets the world know you are a truly stylish girl. Follow these simple steps to create a bold and beautiful bracelet.

You will need:

2 ft of gift ribbon in a pretty color • clean, plastic drinking straws • scraps of gift wrap • scissors • a glue stick

1. Cut your scraps of gift wrap into lots of long triangle shapes with bases about ¼-inch wide. The longer your triangles, the fatter your beads will be, so try to vary their shape so you have some very long triangles and some shorter ones. This will make your bracelet more unique.

2. Turn one of your triangles pattern-side down on a flat surface and apply a thin layer of glue to the wide end.

3. Lay the end of a drinking straw along the wet end of the triangle and press it down gently so that it sticks to the straw.

4. Roll the paper triangle around the straw until you reach the tip. Apply a little glue to the tip of the paper and stick it down.

5. Carefully snip the "bead" off the drinking straw using your scissors.

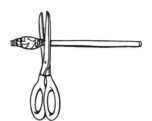

6. Repeat steps **2** to **5** until you have lots of beautiful beads.

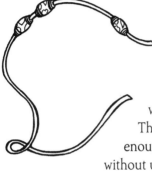

7. Thread your beads onto the ribbon. Stop when you have enough beads on the ribbon to wrap all the way around your wrist. Then add another five beads. This will make your bracelet long enough to slip on and off your hand without undoing it.

8. Tie the bracelet around your wrist and secure it with a double knot and then a bow. This can be quite tricky, so you might want to ask a friend to help.

Fabulous tip: Now that you have your beautiful bracelet, why stop there? You could make one for each of your fabulous friends. Why not make necklaces to go with them? Simply make more beads and use a longer length of ribbon!

mothers day present

27

HOW TO APPEAR COSMOPOLITAN

To be "cosmopolitan" means that you are a stylish lady who has seen the world. However, you don't need to jump on an airplane to make people think that you're a sophisticated jet-setter. Simply sprinkle your speech with some fabulous foreign expressions to add "va-va-voom" to your vocabulary.

FABULOUS FOREIGN PHRASES

Voilà (pronounced *Vwa-la*)–French–means "There it is." Use it when you have completed a project or given a set of instructions to someone or even when you're presenting something to a friend.

C'est la vie (pronounced *Say la vee*)–French–means "That's life." Use it when something hasn't gone exactly according to plan. For added effect, sigh deeply and shrug your shoulders when you say it.

Ciao (pronounced *Chow*)–Italian–can mean "Hello" or "Good-bye." If you're saying it to a girlfriend, add *Bella*, which means "Beautiful," on the end of it to sound even more authentic.

Prego (pronounced *Pray-go*)–Italian–means "You're welcome." Say it right after anyone thanks you.

Hasta mañana (pronounced *A-sta man-yan-a*)–Spanish–means "See you tomorrow." Say it breezily as you leave school.

Fabulous tip: To add a cosmopolitan edge to saying "Hello," greet your friends with an "air kiss" on each cheek. To air-kiss, touch your right cheek to your friend's right cheek and make a "mwah" sound with your lips. Then repeat on the other side.

HOW TO SERVE AFTERNOON TEA

What better way to spend a summer afternoon than by enjoying delicious dainty treats with your most fabulous friends?

SETTING THE TABLE

Cover the table with a pretty tablecloth. A white one with flowers is best if you have one. If you don't, simply cover the table with a bedsheet.

Set the table with a small plate for each guest. Afternoon tea is a dainty affair, so dinner plates should only be used as serving plates in the center of the table and not for eating off of.

SAY IT WITH FLOWERS

Nothing makes a table look lovelier than a simple arrangement of fresh flowers in the center. They don't need to be fancy, just a few sweet peas from the garden or even some dandelions and daisies arranged in a water glass—something to give the feeling of bringing the outdoors in.

TREATS TO EAT

Afternoon tea is more of a snack than a full meal, so make sure your tasty treats are beautifully bite-sized. Sandwiches should be cut into dainty rectangles rather than big triangles, and crusts should be removed (see page 33). Follow these easy recipes to make your afternoon tea the toast of the town.

DELICIOUS ICED TEA

You will need:

4 tea bags • 2 cups boiling water • 1 cup sugar
• 4 ¼ cups cold water • 2 lemons, cut in half • lots of ice

Place the tea bags into a heat-proof pitcher. Pour in the boiling water. Ask an adult to help you with this. Stir the tea bags and water together for about 1 minute. Leave the tea bags in the water for 30 minutes.

After 30 minutes, remove the tea bags and stir in the sugar until it is all dissolved. Make sure your pitcher is big enough to hold the rest of the water and ice plus the sweetened tea. Add the cold water and squeeze in the juice from your lemons. Give your tea a good stir and add the ice. Pour into tall glasses and enjoy.

SUPERB STRAWBERRY SHORTCAKE
You will need:

1 ½ cups plain flour • ¼ cup rice flour
• ½ cup cold butter, cut into small pieces
• ¼ cup sugar • 8 oz sliced strawberries
• ⅔ cup heavy or whipping cream
• 4 whole strawberries to decorate

1. Preheat the oven to 300°F. Ask an adult to help you with this.

2. Grease a 7-inch, loose-bottomed cake pan by dipping a piece of waxed paper in a little butter and rubbing it around the inside of the pan until it is completely covered in a thin layer of grease.

3. Sift the plain flour and rice flour into a large mixing bowl, and add the pieces of butter.

4. Now get your hands into the bowl and rub the butter and flour between your fingertips. As you do this, raise your hands above the bowl and sprinkle the buttery flour back into it. This will mix the flour with the butter and add some air to make your shortcake nice and light.

5. Continue to do this until the mixture resembles fine breadcrumbs. Then stir in the sugar with a wooden spoon.

6. Squeeze the mixture together with your hands to make a ball of dough.

7. Put the dough into your cake pan and press it down with the back of a spoon until it covers the bottom of the pan evenly.

8. Take a butter knife and gently slice the shortcake into eight even wedges to make it easier to cut once it is cooked.

9. Ask an adult to put your shortcake in the oven for 30 minutes.

10. After 30 minutes have an adult help you take the shortcake out of the oven. Sprinkle some sugar on top while it is still in the pan and let it cool.

11. When the shortcake is completely cool, remove it from the pan and separate it into the eight wedges.

12. To finish your fabulous shortcake, whip the cream in a large bowl using a whisk. Whip until the cream forms soft peaks and then stir in the sliced strawberries.

13. Top four wedges with a large dollop of cream. Put the other four wedges on top of the cream and decorate with a smaller dollop of cream.

14. Decorate each slice with a small whole strawberry with the leaf still attached. *Voilà!*

FANTASTIC FINGER SANDWICHES

You will need:

4 slices of wheat bread • 4 slices of white bread
• 2 slices of ham • cream cheese
• thin slices of cucumber

1. Take four slices of wheat bread, and spread one side of each slice with cream cheese.

2. Cover two slices of the bread with slices of cucumber and then sprinkle with a little salt and pepper.

3. Cover the cucumber layer with the two extra slices of wheat bread, cream-cheese side down, just as you would with a normal sandwich, and press them down.

4. Use a butter knife to trim off all the crusts, and then cut your sandwiches into three equal rectangles. You should have six finger sandwiches all together.

5. Repeat this with the white bread, but this time use the slices of ham instead of cucumber.

Fabulous tip: If your mom has fancy dishes that you are allowed to use, choose two pretty plates to display the sandwiches on. Alternatively, you could make the cake stand on page 97.

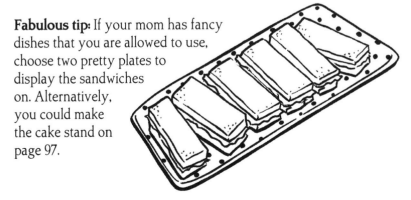

HOW TO MAKE A FABULOUS SUMMER SKIRT

Spruce up your summer wardrobe with this sassy skirt carefully crafted from an old pillowcase—cheap-chic at its best.

You will need:

an old, clean pillowcase • scissors • some newspaper
• a small paintbrush • fabric glue • 6 ft thin ribbon • a safety pin

1. Carefully cut open the closed end of the pillowcase using scissors, and turn it inside out.

2. Fold over 2 inches of fabric all the way around the cut edge, then ask an adult to iron this fold to form a crease.

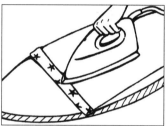

3. Lay down some newspaper to protect your surface, and place a couple of pages inside your pillowcase.

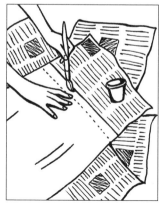

4. Unfold your crease and then, using your paintbrush, apply a thin layer of fabric glue right along the cut edge of one side of your pillowcase. Fold it back down so that it sticks and let it dry.

5. Turn the pillowcase over and repeat step **4** on the other side. This will make the "case" for your drawstring. If your pillowcase has a flap (for tucking the pillow in) at the open end, glue this down as well, using the same method.

6. When your pillowcase is completely dry, turn it right-side out and decide which side you want to be the front.

7. Carefully use your scissors to snip two small slits, about 2 inches apart, in the top of your skirt, just above the seam you have stuck down. Be careful not to snip through to the second layer.

8. Attach the safety pin to the end of your ribbon and push it through one of the slits.

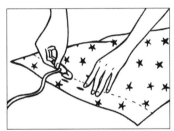

9. Feed the safety pin all the way around the inside of your drawstring case until you can pull it out through the other slit.

10. Pull on your skirt, and tie the ribbon at the front in a pretty bow to hold it up.

Fabulous tip: Don't worry if you don't have a patterned pillowcase. Decorate a plain one with your own design. Practice your pattern on a piece of paper first, then copy it onto your pillowcase using fabric paints, following the directions on the pack.

HOW TO ADDRESS AN AUDIENCE

Picture the scene. You are standing in a crowded room and all of a sudden someone asks you to make a speech in front of everyone. It could be a friend's birthday, a school awards ceremony, or an event with your family. Whatever the occasion, you need to be prepared. Follow these fear-busting tips to help make sure that nerves don't get the better of you, and that your speech is a memorable one.

BEAT THOSE BUTTERFLIES

• Think about the occasion you're speaking at, and make sure you thank the important people before you get started. This might be the birthday girl, the principal of your school, or your mom and dad.

• Making eye contact with members of your audience will give the impression of confidence (it will also help you remember you're surrounded by friendly faces). If you're feeling really nervous, find a friend in the audience and focus on her face—she'll be sure to flash you an encouraging smile.

• Keep it short and sweet. If you haven't had time to prepare anything, then it's best to say a few well-chosen words and leave it at that. Otherwise you'll be in danger of doing some very un-fabulous waffling.

• Stand up straight and try to relax your shoulders. Speak more slowly and clearly than you would normally. It might sound to you as if you're speaking in slow motion, but nerves tend to make people speak faster without realizing it. Keeping it s-l-o-w and clear will make sure that everyone understands every word.

HOW TO GIVE YOUR SKIN A FABULOUS NATURAL GLOW

Forget expensive cosmetics—your young skin has a natural glow that no beauty lotion or potion can copy. Follow these simple rules to make the most of the youthful radiance that all adults long for.

DON'T WASH IT AWAY

As tempting as it is, don't stay too long in a hot bath or shower. While you might think steaming-hot showers are good for you, they actually draw the moisture out of your skin. Skin needs to retain its moisture to look its best.

GET SWEATY

Exercising is not just good for a healthy body, but perfect for great-looking skin, too. Sweating is your body's natural way of eliminating nasty impurities that can clog up the pores of your skin, causing pimples. So what are you waiting for?

FOOD, FABULOUS FOOD

Eating foods rich in vitamins helps skin look its best. Make sure you eat plenty of tomatoes, sweet potatoes, cantaloupe, citrus fruits, spinach, and broccoli. If you can eat fish once or twice a week, such as salmon or tuna, this will also give your skin a natural boost.

CATCH SOME ZZZZZZZZS

Getting enough sleep is a must. Your body repairs itself during sleep so avoid too many late nights. This way your skin will look fresh and radiant, and you'll have bag-free eyes, too!

Fabulous tip: Some scientists believe that eating garlic helps improve the life span of your skin cells. So ask your parents to cook with it a few times a week. Apparently, garlic keeps vampires at bay, too—another reason to sleep well at night.

HOW TO MAKE A NEW YORK–STYLE BRUNCH

Brunch is the perfect treat for fabulous friends who are feeling hungry after a sleepover. It is the equivalent of a late breakfast or an early lunch, so your guests should be up, dressed, and ready for the day.

You will need:
(to serve four)

4 bagels, cut in half • 6 eggs • ¼ cup milk • salt and pepper • 1 tablespoon butter • 4 slices of ham or smoked salmon

1. Crack your eggs into a bowl by tapping each one against the rim of the bowl until it breaks open and then pull the shells apart. Remove any pieces of shell that fall into the bowl.

2. Beat the eggs using a fork until all the yolks are broken and you can't see any of the clear, white parts. Add salt and pepper and stir in the milk. Put the bowl to one side.

3. Toast your bagels in the toaster one at a time and keep them warm in the oven, set to a low heat. Ask an adult for help.

4. Melt the butter in a saucepan over medium heat. Ask an adult to help you with this, too.

5. When the butter has melted, pour in the eggs and stir with a wooden spoon. The eggs will begin to cook and set, so keep stirring to stop them from sticking to the bottom of the pan.

6. When your eggs are light and fluffy and there is no runny egg left in the pan, remove them from the heat.

7. Take your bagels out of the oven, and place the bottom half of each one on a plate. Spoon a quarter of your eggs onto each bagel.

8. Place a slice of ham or smoked salmon on top of the eggs, and then place the top onto each of the bagels. Serve with a cool glass of orange juice. Yum!

HOW TO AVOID WRINKLES

You might think that you don't need to worry about getting wrinkles until you're much older. However, you can take action right now that will help keep your skin smooth and fabulously wrinkle-free in the future.

• The biggest cause of wrinkles is the sun. To protect the delicate skin of your face against the sun's rays, wear suntan lotion with an SPF (this stands for "Sun Protection Factor") of at least 30. Use it every day, not just in the summer when you are at the beach.

• Use a grainy facial scrub once a week. The small grains will remove any bits of dead skin on the surface of your face and leave your complexion looking fresh and smooth. This process is called "exfoliation."

• Did you know that the food you eat has a direct impact on your skin? There are certain foods that are great at battling the signs of aging. Spinach, blueberries, carrots, and red peppers are all fabulous "wrinkle warriors." Eating turkey will keep your skin feeling firm and, best of all, dark chocolate has been proven to fight wrinkles, too. Hooray!

HOW TO HAVE THE MOST FABULOUSLY SMOOTH SKIN

Did you know that your body is covered in yucky dead skin cells? The key to smooth skin is removing these skin cells and locking the moisture into your skin to keep it supple and to keep it from drying out.

SALT OF THE EARTH SCRUB

You can buy body scrubs, otherwise known as "exfoliants," which will sweep dead skin away, but these can be expensive. Why spend money when you can make them at home?

You will need:

a small bowl • 3 tablespoons sea salt
• 3 tablespoons olive oil
• a few drops of essential oil

1. Spoon the salt into a mixing bowl and crush up the larger pieces with your fingers.

2. Pour in the olive oil and add a few drops of your chosen essential oil. If you plan to use your scrub in the morning, try using lemon, grapefruit, or eucalyptus oil as these will help to wake you up. If you are planning to use it in the evening, sweet lavender or rose oils are perfect as they can help to ease you into a blissful sleep. Stir the ingredients together.

APPLY YOURSELF

Apply your scrub to damp or wet skin—in the shower is ideal. Rub it into your skin gently, using circular motions to help increase the circulation of blood in your skin. Concentrate on areas of rougher skin, such as your knees and elbows and your heels. Rinse off with warm water.

HOW TO MOISTURIZE

Now that you have scrubbed away all of the dead skin cells, you need to lock in all of your skin's precious moisture.

Apply moisturizer to your body immediately after showering or bathing, while your skin is still damp. Squeeze out a blob about the size of a dime into your palm. Dip the fingertips of your other hand into this blob and start moisturizing your body at your feet, using both hands. Move in a sweeping motion up one leg at a time. Only use more lotion once all of the first blob has been rubbed in.

Once you have moisturized your whole body, let the lotion sink in for about two minutes. Dust yourself with a little baby powder to help lock in the moisture. Perfection!

HOW TO MAKE AN ANTIQUE SILVER TRINKET BOX

Even your most treasured trinkets can make the surfaces in your bedroom look messy. Tuck away your special collectibles in this stylish box, essential for every girl's dresser.

You will need:

a box with a lid • a sheet of thin cardstock • some string
• white glue • scissors • tinfoil • a paintbrush
• a Q-tip • a pencil

1. Use your pencil to draw some small shapes onto the sheet of cardstock and then cut them out. You might decide to use heart shapes for a romantic look or perhaps circles and squares for a more geometric design.

2. Arrange the shapes on the lid of your box in a pretty pattern. Carefully cut out more shapes if you need them. Try layering shapes on top of each other to add more depth to your design. Then stick them down and let the glue dry.

3. To make your design even more special, glue some string around each part of your pattern. For example, if it is hearts, glue string around the outline of each heart.

4. When the lid is completely dry, cover it with a thin layer of glue using a paintbrush. Make sure you spread the glue into all of the nooks and crannies of your design.

5. Tear off a sheet of tinfoil that is large enough to cover the box lid and wrap around its rim.

6. Lay the sheet of foil over the lid and press it down onto your design. Carefully pick out the details of your design by smoothing the foil over it with your fingertips. (Don't fold it over the rim yet.)

7. Use a Q-tip to rub the foil around the shapes and the string you glued on to make sure you get into all the nooks and crannies.

8. When your design is outlined clearly by the foil, spread some more glue around the sides of the lid. Carefully fold the foil down over the sides. Tear away any excess.

9. Repeat steps **1** through **8** to decorate the base of your box. This time glue your shapes around the sides. When you add the foil, the sides of your box may look more wrinkled than the lid, but this will add to the antique effect.

10. When both the lid and base of your box are completely dry, put your treasures inside.

Fabulous tip: If you don't want your box to be silver, use acrylic paints in any colors you like to cover the foil on the lid and base. Let them dry thoroughly before putting your treasures inside.

HOW TO STAND OUT FROM A CROWD

Everybody wants to feel like they fit in, but if you want to be truly fabulous, blending into the background isn't an option.

LOOK THE PART

Dressing the same as your friends means you will always be grouped together and compared to one another. Make your look a little different by adding accessories, such as a silk scarf threaded through the belt loops of your jeans (see page 112) and some funky jewelry.

You could even change the way you style your hair. You don't have to go crazy and dye your hair green. Keep it simple. If your friends all wear their hair in high ponytails, wear yours in a low one arranged over one shoulder.

TAKE A STAND

Don't just agree with your friends for the sake of it. If you don't share the same views, don't be afraid to say so. Not having the same opinion doesn't mean you can't be friends. A real friend will respect you for being different even when she doesn't agree with you—but make sure you respect her opinions, too.

GET A HOBBY

Find a new and exciting hobby. Listening to a different type of music, reading books by different authors, or doing something you've never done before, such as joining a local drama group, can be great fun. It will give you something interesting to talk about, and you might make some new friends along the way.

HOW TO SIGN AN AUTOGRAPH

Being as fabulous as you are is sure to attract you a few fans. Follow the tips below to make signing autographs a breeze!

YOUR SIGNATURE STYLE

Choose a writing style that suits your name. If you have a short name, make every letter count with bold swirls. If you have a long name, adding lots of swirls and detail will make it difficult to repeat every time, so concentrate on the first letters of your first and last name and trail off from there in a mysterious squiggle.

PRACTICE MAKES PERFECT

Practice your signature over and over again on a sheet of blank paper. It should flow naturally so that you don't need to think about it.

Fabulous tip: To speed things up a bit, shorten your name like "RPatz" and "JLo." This will keep your wrist from getting sore.

HOW TO WRITE YOUR FIRST NOVEL

Picture this—you are sitting behind a table surrounded by books with your name printed in shining gold ink on the covers. Eager fans are lining up around the block to meet you and ask you to sign a copy of your fabulous first novel. If you want to know how to make this dream a reality, read on . . .

DARE TO DREAM

Do you sometimes wish that life could be more exciting? Do you find yourself daydreaming about weird and wonderful things happening? Why not tap into this creative part of your brain and turn these dreams into your first novel?

Becoming a novelist takes dedication and patience, but follow these handy hints and you'll soon be on your way to a best seller.

THE "WRITE" QUESTIONS

Who? The first thing to think about is your hero or heroine. Why not base this character on yourself? Have you always wanted to be fearless or to be able to fly or to be a famous ballerina? Now is your chance!

What? Decide what your hero or heroine wants to achieve. Who or what is standing in the way?

Where and when? Decide where your novel takes place. It could be in your hometown, in a famous ballet school, or in an imaginary world full of mythical creatures that have superpowers—you are in control.

KEEP THE READER IN SUSPENSE

Whether your story ends in triumph or tragedy is up to you, but try not to give away the ending too soon. Distract your readers' attention away from the main plot by introducing something called a "cliff-hanger." When something dramatic happens in your story, change direction—leave the hero or heroine in some kind of terrible danger, such as dangling from the edge of a cliff.

"Deep in the dungeon, the ferocious, three-headed dog approached, with his enormous eyes bulging.

Meanwhile, outside the castle, her pony chewed on a big, juicy apple . . ."

This will keep your readers turning the pages to find out what happens in the end.

OVER THE RAINBOW

All stories need to have a beginning, a middle, and an end. Imagine your story as an arc, like a rainbow. Start at one end of the arc—this is your beginning. Build up to the highest point of your arc, which is the middle, where the most exciting things happen. Finally, follow the arc back down to ground level, the end of your novel, where everything needs to be finished and all loose ends need to be tied up.

NOVEL IDEAS

• **Do** carry a notebook with you wherever you go, so you'll always be prepared when inspiration strikes. Remember that your novel will grow over time, and you won't get all your answers in one day.

• **Don't** feel like you have to use all of your good ideas in your first novel. They might not all work together. You can always save some for the sequels.

• **Do** ask your friends or family to read your work. Listening to other people's opinions will help take your story in directions that you maybe hadn't thought of.

• **Don't** get upset if you receive criticism. Take any advice on board and be prepared to rewrite your story to make it the best it can be.

HOW TO PLAY THE "FABULOUS-YOU" GAME

Everybody has days when they feel far from fabulous and could use a little boost. Who better to help you out in tough times than one of your best friends? Get together and play this game to remind yourselves just how wonderful you both are.

You will need:

2 notebooks • 2 pens • a good friend
• somewhere private and comfortable to sit
• a timer

1. On the left-hand side of a page in your notebook, list the following: "Appearance," "Fashion sense," "Personality," "Fun factor," "You have helped me when . . . ," "You are fabulous because . . . ," "If I had all the money in the world

I would buy you . . . ," and "If there was one thing I could change about me to be more like you, I would change . . ." Have your friend do the same.

2. Set the timer for ten minutes. You and your friend should go to different corners of the room to fill in your sheet.

3. Work your way down the list, thinking about all the things that are most fabulous about your friend. Try to list the qualities that make her special or unique.

4. When the timer goes off, finish what you were writing. Trade lists with your friend as if you were grading each other's homework.

5. Read your lists, putting a check next to things you agree with and a question mark next to anything you don't understand.

6. When you have finished reading, go through your lists together and explain your answers.

How good does it feel to have someone think all those lovely things about you? If someone else can see all of those good qualities in you and likes you for them, then you should value yourself, too!

HOW TO MAKE A FABULOUS BIRDBATH

Birds love a good bath—somewhere safe where they can clean their feathers and have a drink. Keep the birds in your garden looking their best with an easy-to-make birdbath—the perfect place for feathered friends to freshen up after a long flight.

You will need:

3 terra-cotta flowerpots in 3 different sizes
• a terra-cotta plant tray
• a handful of gravel and some stones • water

1. Choose a nice, safe spot to place your birdbath. It should be out in the open, so that your feathered friends have a good view of any pesky cats approaching.

2. When you have picked the spot, you can make the pedestal of the birdbath. Turn the largest plant pot upside down and place the next-smallest pot on top of it so that it fits snugly over the bottom of the pot below.

3. Now turn the smallest pot upside down and fit this over the bottom of the medium-sized pot.

4. Take your plant tray and sit this on top of the smallest pot to make the bath for your birds to splash around in.

5. Place a couple of handfuls of gravel and some stones in the bottom of your tray. This will help any small creatures that find their way inside the tray to climb out again. It will also make the base of the bath less slippery for the birds.

6. Now all you need to do is fill the birdbath with some water from the tap and wait for the birds to discover their new oasis. Keep a bird book handy so you can identify them as they fly in to spruce themselves up.

7. Don't forget to check your birdbath regularly to make sure the water is clean and fresh. The rain should keep it filled up, but if you see it is dry, add some water.

Fabulous tip: Don't be tempted to paint the birdbath bright colors. This will discourage birds from using it.

Warning: Take your birdbath apart when there is bad weather since it could fall over and break.

HOW TO MAKE YOUR HAIR WORK FOR YOU

It goes without saying that it should be you letting your hair down, not your hair letting you down. Instead of just pulling it back into a ponytail, follow these tips to make your hair your crowning glory.

• Get a good haircut from a professional stylist. Cut out pictures from magazines of people whose hair you admire and take them along with you to the salon.

• Ask your stylist which style would suit you and your hair best, and listen to her advice. She will consider your face shape, type of hair, and the way it falls, and she'll come up with the best style to suit you.

• Be honest with your stylist about how much styling you are prepared to do to keep your hair looking fabulous. If you want something you can just wash and go, let her know.

• When your stylist has finished cutting, watch carefully how she dries and styles your hair. That way you will know how to create that salon look at home.

• The more you practice styling your hair, the easier it will get. Soon you will be styling your hair in moments and getting great results every time.

HOW TO MAKE YOUR OWN LOVE-HEART HAIR CLIPS

Buying pretty hair clips can get expensive, and this makes it especially annoying if a friend turns up wearing the same ones. These hair clips are so easy to make that you could make a set to go with every outfit. No one will have clips quite like yours!

You will need:

felt in two different colors • a plain, snap hair clip
• a bead • paper • a pencil • a felt-tip pen • scissors
• 3 ft of sewing thread • a needle

1. Lay a sheet of paper over the heart shapes above, and trace around them using a pencil. Carefully cut out both hearts.

2. Lay one of your hearts onto your felt and draw around it with a felt-tip pen. Do the same with the other heart on the other piece of felt. Carefully cut out both hearts.

3. Lay the smaller heart on top of the bigger heart and place a bead on top of them. Position them how you want them to sit on your hair clip.

4. Thread your needle and pull the thread so that the ends meet. Tie a knot in the end so that your needle is attached to a loop of thread and can't come off.

5. Pick up your pile of hearts and bead and push the needle through the center from the back to the front. Keep pushing the needle so that it passes through the large heart, the small heart, and then thread it through the bead on top. Push the needle back through the hearts once you are through to the other side of the bead.

6. Turn your hearts upside down and lay them on the top side of your hair clip. Pass the needle through the hair clip and around the central metal tab. Then push it back through the back of the hearts and through the bead again.

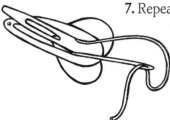

7. Repeat this stitch ten times until the heart is securely attached to the clip. Finish with the needle at the back of the clip.

8. Carefully cut the thread leaving about 2 inches hanging loose. Tie these ends in a knot to secure your stitches. Trim the loose threads.

9. Simply sweep your hair to one side and secure it with your hair clip. Repeat these steps to make as many clips as you need to complete your look.

Fabulous tip: Why stop at hearts? Experiment with different shapes, beads, and fabrics. These clips make fabulous gifts for your friends when made in their favorite colors.

HOW TO BANISH BOREDOM FOREVER

"Only boring people are bored." Adults love saying this, but funnily enough it is true. Fill your free time with fun activities, and you will never need to hear those infuriating five words ever again.

CHANGE YOUR ATTITUDE

The first thing to do is adopt a "P.M.A."–meaning a "Positive Mental Attitude." Look at free time as a fabulous opportunity to do something fun and enjoy some quality "you" time. Follow these tips to get yourself going.

• **Get up.** Sitting around doing nothing will only make you feel miserable and even more bored.

• **Get moving.** As soon as you start feeling bored, try to do some exercise. Exercise is a great way to lift your spirits and get yourself in the mood to find something fabulous to do. Why not create your own dance routine in your room or learn how to twirl a baton (see page 93)?

• **Get fabulous.** View free time as an opportunity to make yourself even more fabulous than you already are. Reading books and listening to new music are great ways to relax and pass the time and will give you something interesting to talk about the next time you see your friends.

COUNTING THE DAYS

Check your calendar to see if there are any friends' birthdays coming up—you may need to make a birthday card or present for them. Homemade gifts are so much more personal. If you have time, you could even make yourself a little something.

CALL FOR HELP

Do you feel sociable? Maybe you could call a few friends to see if they want some company, too.

HOW TO MAKE A SOPHISTICATED SUMMER SALAD

This salad looks and tastes amazing and is very easy to make.

You will need:

4 big, ripe tomatoes • olive oil
• salt and ground black pepper • 10 oz mozzarella cheese
• 8 large basil leaves

1. Carefully use a butter knife to cut the tomatoes into slices about ½ inch thick. You may want to ask an adult for help.

2. Arrange the slices around the edge of a dinner plate. When you have completed the circle, arrange more slices in a smaller circle inside the larger one, overlapping the slices already there. Continue until the plate is covered with tomatoes.

3. Drizzle the plate with olive oil by positioning your clean thumb over the opening of the bottle and allowing just a little oil to come out in a thin stream. Sprinkle with salt and ground black pepper.

4. Tear the mozzarella into bite-sized pieces and arrange them on top of the tomatoes.

5. Tear the basil leaves into thin strips and sprinkle them over the salad before serving. Delicious!

HOW TO MAKE A TROPICAL BATH TREAT

What better way to warm up during the winter than with a long soak in the bath? Harsh winds and central heating can leave your skin looking dull and lifeless, so make yourself a tropical skin treat with a moisturizing milk bath. It's time to lie back and dream of paradise . . .

You will need:

1 small can coconut milk
• 1 cup powdered milk • ½ cup avocado oil

1. Carefully open the can of coconut milk using a can opener and pour the contents into a medium-sized bowl.

2. Scrape out all the stubborn bits of creamy coconut from the can using a spoon.

3. Add the powdered milk and stir thoroughly.

4. Add the avocado oil and mix again.

5. Pour your tropical treat into a small pitcher and add it to your warm bath.

Fabulous tip: Set the mood with some relaxing tropical music or rainforest sounds. Your skin will be silky smooth, and you'll feel like a queen. Pure bliss.

HOW TO MAKE
PERSONALIZED STATIONERY

A girl is only as stylish as her stationery, and what better
way to stay in touch than with your own beautifully headed
notepaper? No e-mail or text message will ever be as fabulous
as a stylishly handwritten letter.

You will need:

scrap paper • a sharp pencil
• a pad of plain, white paper (8 ½ x 11 is best) • a ruler
• a black pen • an eraser
• a photocopier (at your local library, for instance)
• a piece of lined paper (8 ½ x 11)

1. Take a sheet of scrap paper and a pencil and, in your most
fabulous writing, write your name and address like so:

Miss (Your name)
(1st line of your address)
(2nd line of your address)
(The town you live in)
(Your zip code)

Practice this on scrap paper until it looks just right.

2. Take a sheet of plain, white paper and use your ruler
to measure 1 inch down from the top edge. Mark this with
your pencil and then use this mark to draw a horizontal line
parallel to the top edge of the page.

3. Use your pencil to write your name in the middle of the
line you have just drawn, and then write the rest of your
address underneath as you did on your scrap paper.

4. Now you need to select a "motif"—a small picture—to decorate your paper. Choose something that reflects your personality or one of your hobbies. There are some sample pictures you could use as a guide on page 64.

5. To use one of these pictures, simply place your piece of paper over the page and position the picture where you would like it to appear—directly under your zip code or in the bottom right-hand corner look best. Trace around the outline of the picture using your pencil.

6. When you are happy with your design, trace over your address and your motif very carefully with your black pen so that it will photocopy well.

7. Erase your pencil marks, including the line you drew at the top of the page.

8. You now have what is called a "master copy." Photocopy it as many times as you like to make the rest of your stationery.

MARVELOUS MOTIFS

9. Keep your master copy somewhere safe and do not use it for writing your letters on. You can use it again to create as much new paper as you like—if you use it to write on, you will have to start all over again.

10. Now you are ready to write your letter. To help with this, take your sheet of lined paper and line your ruler up with the top line on the page. Using your black pen, draw along this line. Repeat this for all the lines on the page.

11. Before you write a letter, put a piece of personalized stationery over the lined paper. You should be able to see the lines you have just drawn through the page. Use these lines as a guide as you write so your letter will be super neat and tidy.

Fabulous tip: Why not put some colored paper into the photocopier to make a more dramatic statement? Just make sure your master copy is white, or it won't photocopy well.

HOW TO MAKE A SPA TREATMENT FOR YOUR FACE

The rich and famous spend lots of money on skin-care products formulated especially for their skin types by teams of experts. Follow the tips below to discover your skin type and then make your own spa treatment.

WHAT IS YOUR SKIN TYPE?

Touch your face. If it feels rough and tight rather than soft and supple, then it is likely that you have dry skin. Dry skin lacks moisture. This can make it look dull and lifeless. To check, take a piece of adhesive tape and apply it to your skin. If the tape is covered in flakes of skin when you peel it off, then you have dry skin.
Go to treatment A.

If your skin is prone to rashes or burns easily in the sun, then you have sensitive skin.
Go to treatment B.

If your skin is usually shiny and you are prone to getting a few pimples, take a sheet of toilet paper and hold it to your face. If it feels as though it would stick or if your skin leaves dark patches on the paper, then you have oily skin.
Go to treatment C.

TREATMENT A: AVO-CADABRA!

This face mask is a cheap, natural, but effective way to help moisturize dry skin. Avocados are rich in vitamin E, which really helps to soothe itchiness and smooth away flakiness.

You will need:

half an avocado • 3 tablespoons honey

1. Spoon the inside of the avocado out into a bowl and mash it to a gooey pulp using a fork.

2. Add the honey and mix together well.

3. Wash your face like you usually do. Then pat it dry with a towel.

4. Apply the mixture to your face using your fingers, leaving an area 1 inch around each eye uncovered. Leave it on your skin for 15 minutes.

5. Rinse with warm water. Pat dry.

Fabulous tip: It is important to drink water on a regular basis to replenish moisture in the skin, so drink up!

TREATMENT B: HONEY BEE-AUTIFUL

Honey is a great natural ingredient for sensitive skin because it has calming properties that help soothe irritation and redness.

You will need:

4 tablespoons honey
• 1 tablespoon hot water

1. Spoon the honey into a bowl and add the hot water.

2. Stir well and apply the mixture to your face using your fingers, leaving about 1 inch uncovered around each eye. Leave on for 15 minutes before rinsing off with warm water.

Fabulous tip: Be careful with sensitive skin. Experimenting with different ingredients can cause a rash. Make sure you only buy products marked "hypoallergenic"–they have been tested to make sure they won't cause a rash in most cases.

TREATMENT C: LEMON MERINGUE MAGIC

Absorb excess oils with this zesty refresher.

You will need:

1 egg white • 6 drops lemon juice
• 6 drops distilled witch hazel (available at the pharmacy)

1. Whisk the egg white until it is foamy and stiff.

2. Stir in the witch hazel and lemon juice very gently so that you don't burst the bubbles in the foam.

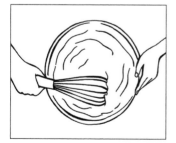

3. Gently apply to your face with your fingertips, avoiding an area 1 inch around each eye. Let dry for about 15 minutes and then rinse off with warm water.

HOW TO TURN YOUR BEDROOM INTO A HAVEN

Your bedroom says a lot about you, so you want to make sure you are sending out the right message to any visitors. Follow these tips so that anyone who sees your bedroom will know immediately that it belongs to a truly fabulous girl.

GET THINGS STRAIGHT

Your room needs to be a haven for you to escape to, not a pit you want to escape from. Getting things looking neat will create the illusion of space and make your room seem much larger than it is.

• **Do** throw it away. Trash unwanted stuff, not your room, that is. Be brutal with items you no longer need—either throw them out or ask an adult to drop them off at a thrift store. The fewer things you have, the fewer things you have to clean up.

• **Do** have a place for everything.

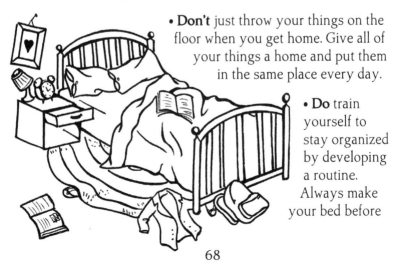

• **Don't** just throw your things on the floor when you get home. Give all of your things a home and put them in the same place every day.

• **Do** train yourself to stay organized by developing a routine. Always make your bed before you leave for school. Pile clean clothes on your bed so that you will have to put them away before you can get into bed at night.

GET FABULOUS

These simple touches will add a fresh feel to your room.

• Tie back your curtains with wide, colored ribbons so they frame your windows nicely. Choose ribbon that goes with the colors already in your room, or make a bold statement and go for bright, contrasting shades.

• To add a splash of color to your desk and brighten up homework blues, nothing beats a bouquet of flowers. Fresh flowers are best, but you can use silk or paper flowers instead. Choose blooms that reflect your style—go cute and girly with roses and lilies, or bold and quirky with bright sunflowers, tulips, or orchids.

• Hang a string of twinkling lights over your bed to make a canopy any princess would be proud of. You'll be sure to feel relaxed surrounded by sparkling lights.

• Add that personal touch by putting up a few pictures. Choose either photos of your friends and family or your favorite place or animal, or just pictures you like from a magazine. Simply put them into old picture frames and hang them on your wall.

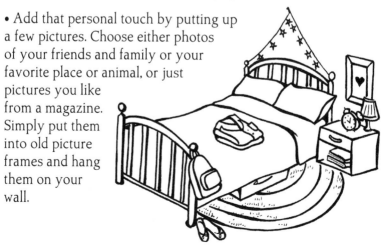

Fabulous tip: If your room feels a little on the small side, hang a large mirror opposite your window. The mirror will double the amount of light in your room during the daytime, making it feel much bigger than it actually is.

HOW TO MAKE A FABULOUS SUPERSTAR SCRAPBOOK

Following the career of your favorite star can be fun, but all your pictures and clippings can look messy. What better way to display pictures and articles about your favorite star than with your very own scrapbook made in his or her honor?

You will need:

a pack of colored 8 ½ x 11 cardstock
• a pencil • a hole puncher
• a glue stick • felt-tip pens
• an 8 ½ x 11 plastic sheet protector (hole-punched)
• colored ribbon
• a collection of pictures torn from magazines, old movie tickets, pictures from the Internet
• pretty gift wrap
• sequins and glitter

GET SCRAPPING

Gather all of the pictures of your chosen star and any articles you can find from magazines and newspapers. Ask your friends if they have any pictures they can spare. You could trade them for pictures of their favorite star. See if there are any good pictures of your star on the Internet and ask your parents if you can print some out.

Make sure to keep ticket stubs from any trips you make to the movies to see your star or any concerts you go to. Keep an eye out for anything that may have his or her picture on it.

FULLY BOOKED

1. Take two sheets of cardstock and punch two holes along the center left-hand border. These will form the front and back covers of your scrapbook.

2. Look through your scraps and find an article that has your star's name written in bold letters. Carefully cut out these letters and arrange them on the cover any way you like.

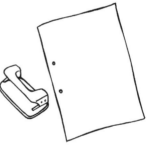

3. Carefully cut a star shape out of your gift wrap and lay this under the name of your star. Paste a photograph of your star on top of the star shape.

4. Take another three sheets of cardstock and punch holes in them in the same places as your front and back covers. Lay these sheets out in front of you.

KEY THEMES

5. Now it is time to theme your pages. Look through your clippings and see if any themes spring to mind, for example; "I like him/her best when . . . ," "He/she is great because . . . ," "His/her favorite things are . . ." Write your themes on the top left-hand side of each sheet of cardstock.

6. Arrange your clippings on the pages by theme. Don't worry if one of your pages doesn't have many clippings. You can always add to it as your collection grows. If some of your clippings don't seem to fit under any of your themes, put these to one side.

7. Carefully cut out key words from the magazines, such as "love," "gorgeous," or "star," to place around your pictures, or write them yourself in a felt-tip pen. When you are happy with your layout, glue the words and pictures into place.

ADD SOME SPARKLE

8. Decorate your pages with sequins and glitter and pictures of things your star likes. If you know what his or her favorite food is, find a picture of it and stick it in.

9. Meanwhile, gather the rest of your clippings and scraps and slip them neatly inside the plastic sheet protector. Place the sheet protector on top of your back cover with the holes on the left-hand side.

10. Collect and pile the rest of your pages on top of the plastic sheet protector. Place the cover page on top.

11. Loop the ribbon through the holes to tie the pages together. Tie a pretty bow at the front. Flip through your scrapbook to make sure that the pages will turn easily. If they don't, undo your bow and tie it again with a bit more slack.

12. Each time you need to add a new page, just take some more cardstock and punch holes in the same places, then insert them into the book by untying the ribbon.

Fabulous tip: You don't have to stop at one scrapbook—you can make as many as you like for different things. Why not make one about your favorite animals or your most fabulous friends? Why not create a scrapbook all about your mom and give it to her as a special Mother's Day gift?

HOW TO BE YOUR OWN PERSONAL TRAINER

A personal trainer is someone who motivates people to get in shape and then helps them stay that way. The rich and famous spend a fortune hiring people to do this for them. Why not get one step ahead by learning how to motivate yourself into working out, however and whenever it suits you?

SET A GOAL

Think about what you would like to achieve. Perhaps you would like to be able to run faster, be more flexible, or even just be able to make it through gym class without getting out of breath.

Write your goal down on a piece of paper. Add a sentence describing how it will make you feel when you achieve this goal. Hang this sheet up on your wall.

GET WITH THE PROGRAM

Create a routine, called a "program," that you need to complete three times a week. To make it easier to motivate yourself, pick an exercise you enjoy–this might be taking a brisk walk with your friends or making up some dance moves in your bedroom.

Not all habits are bad. Fitness experts say you need to have completed your routine 23 times (not all at once) in order for it to become a habit. Mark off the times you have completed your routine on a calendar, and give yourself a special treat when you reach number 23.

A FABULOUS WARM-UP

Exercising cold muscles can lead to injury. Start by jogging up and down in place for a minute, and then do these simple stretches to make sure you are nice and warm.

THE THIGH LIFT

These leg lifts are great for working your inner thighs!

1. Lie on your left side with your hand under your head and your right arm stopping you from rolling forward. Bend your right knee at a right angle so that your foot is in line with your left knee.

2. Leaning on your right arm, raise your left leg from the hip, keeping your leg straight, and then lower it gently.

3. Repeat this eight times, then roll over and do the same on the other side with the other leg.

THE DONKEY KICK

This exercise is great for warming up your butt and thighs.

1. Get onto all fours with your knees directly under your hips and your hands directly under your shoulders.

2. Swing your right knee in toward your chest and then push it out behind you, so that your thigh is in line with your back and your foot is directly above your knee.

3. Repeat this eight times, then switch legs.

THE SCISSORS

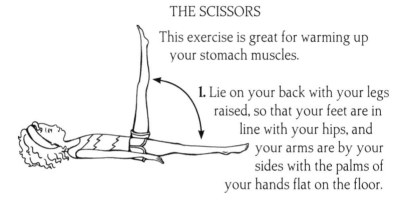

This exercise is great for warming up your stomach muscles.

1. Lie on your back with your legs raised, so that your feet are in line with your hips, and your arms are by your sides with the palms of your hands flat on the floor.

2. Lower your left leg until it almost touches the floor, then raise it again.

3. Repeat this eight times, then switch legs. Now that you are warmed up, you can start your fabulous workout.

Fabulous tip: Choose music with a good beat to work out to. Picking your favorite songs is sure to put you in the "zone."

AFTER YOUR WORKOUT

Remember to "cool down," which means allowing your muscles to relax gradually after a workout. Go for a walk or a gentle jog around the block. Stretch your arms above your head and then touch your toes. Well done. You did it!

HOW TO STOP A STYLE STEALER

Some people say that imitation is the sincerest form of flattery, but it can be very annoying when someone is following your every fashion move.

HOW TO SPOT A COPYCAT

• Has your friend recently started wearing her hair in the same style as you?

• Does she always ask where you bought something and then turn up wearing exactly the same outfit the next time you see her?

If the answer is "Yes" to either question, then you are dealing with a copycat. As irritating as this is, you need to tread very carefully to avoid hurting your friend's feelings.

Compliment your friend every time she wears something different than you. This will make her feel better about herself and more confident about her own style choices.

If this doesn't work, speak to your friend and let her know how you feel. She will probably be very surprised that she has upset you. Be gentle— she is a friend, after all.

Fabulous tip: Why not spend time together making unique homemade accessories? That way you can both be fashionable without having to look exactly the same.

HOW TO MAKE A SWEET BOUQUET

Everybody likes candy, and here is a way to make it even more fabulous. Transform a bag of sweets into a beautiful bouquet.

You will need:

5 wooden skewers • scissors • marshmallows
• gummy candy • a rubber band • a sheet of tissue paper
• adhesive tape • 24 inches of ribbon

1. Carefully use a pair of scissors to cut the pointy ends off the wooden skewers. This can be a bit tricky, so ask an adult for help.

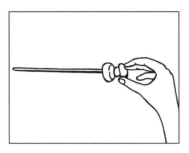

2. Take a wooden skewer and push the end through one of the marshmallows. Keep pushing until the marshmallow sits 1 ½ inches down the skewer.

3. Do the same with one of the colored gummies, pushing it all the way down the skewer until it sits next to the marshmallow.

4. As you add your last gummy candy, push it so that the skewer only goes halfway through the gummy candy. Repeat this for the other four skewers.

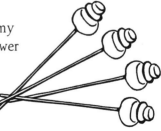

5. Using the rubber band, tie the five skewers together a little way up from their bases to form a bouquet. Adjust the skewers until they form a nice bunch.

6. Take the tissue paper and wrap the candy as though wrapping a bouquet of flowers. Do this by putting your bouquet across the bottom left-hand corner of the paper and rolling the paper around it. Secure with a piece of tape.

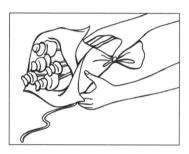

7. Tie the gift ribbon around the bottom of your bouquet, finishing it off with a beautiful bow.

Fabulous tip: For a healthier treat, why not use fruit? Cubes of kiwi, strawberries, and star fruit look fabulous bunched together in a beautiful bouquet. Just replace the tissue paper with tinfoil.

HOW TO BE A FABULOUS FUND-RAISER

Nothing will make you feel more fabulous than raising money for a good cause. Get your friends and family together and hold a bring-and-buy sale.

ONE MONTH TO GO

• Choose the date for your sale. More people will be able to attend on a Saturday or a Sunday. The summertime is best because the weather should be good.

• Choose a venue. If you don't have a front yard, ask a friend or family member if you can hold your sale in theirs.

• A bring-and-buy sale is a great opportunity to get rid of items you no longer need. Look through all of your old things and ask your family to do the same.

• Let people know about your sale. If you allow yourself a month to prepare, this gives other people a chance to think about what they would like to donate to the sale. Make sure people know only to bring items that are clean and that work properly. Nobody is going to buy an old, dirty T-shirt or a jigsaw puzzle with pieces missing.

ONE WEEK TO GO

• Advertise your sale. Make a poster to let people know about it. Say where it is going to be and when. Give details about which charity it is for. When you are happy with your poster, photocopy it and hang copies up around town (remember to remove them after the sale).

• Check that you have lots of coins to give people change on the day of the sale. Ask an adult if they would be willing to change some money into coins.

ON THE DAY OF THE SALE

• Set up your sale a couple of hours before the start time. Arrange the tables so it is easy for people to walk around them and browse the items. Display your items neatly. If you have too much to display on your tables, lay the extra things out on blankets in front of them.

• As people arrive, take their donated items and put them out with the rest.

THE PRICE IS RIGHT

The goal is to make as much money for your chosen charity as possible. However, make sure you don't price your items too highly or people may not buy anything at all. Keep your pricing simple by marking all similar items with the same amount.

T-shirts–$1.50

Coats and jackets–$4.00

Paperback books–.50¢ or 3 for $1.00

Hardcover books–$1.50 or 3 for $4.00

Small toys–$1.00

Larger toys or games–$3.00

You want to sell as many of the items as you can, so toward the end of your sale, cut prices on remaining items by half.

AFTER YOUR SALE

Bag up all the items that are not sold during the sale and take them to your local thrift store.

Count all the money you have collected and give it to an adult. Ask them if they would be so kind as to write a check for the total amount and send it to your chosen charity by mail. Make sure you send it with a letter giving the charity your name and address and the details of your sale. You could even include a photo from your event!

HOW TO LOOK FABULOUS FOR GYM CLASS

Looking good is at the top of every fabulous girl's agenda, even during gym class. You want to look your best for the cameras when you score the winning goal, right?

FIX YOUR HAIR

First, you need to keep your hair away from your face. If you have long hair, a neat mid to high ponytail will create a really sporty look. If you have shorter hair, a hair elastic or headband will also give the illusion that you mean business on the field.

FACE FACTS

A clean face (that means one without makeup) is always best for sports. It's fine to wear some tinted lip balm, but leave it at that.

COOL CLOTHES

You don't need to deviate from the school gym uniform to look good. Looking cool at school is all about your attitude. Understand that your school gym uniform is a fact of life, and be cool enough to accept it. That way you'll ooze confidence rather than looking like you're trying too hard.

Fabulous tip: Keep your school gym uniform clean and fresh by taking it home at least once a week to be washed.

HOW TO MAKE YOUR OWN DESIGNER HANDBAG

All fabulous girls love to wear the latest trends, and a "must-have" handbag is the perfect item to show your friends that you are a style leader and not a fashion follower.

You will need:

a clean pair of old jeans • scissors • 3 ft of thread
• a needle—strong enough to go through denim
• an old belt • a long scarf
• sequins, beads, or buttons to decorate • fabric glue

1. Turn your jeans inside out and cut the legs off at the top of the legs. They will then resemble a very short skirt.

2. Thread your needle and tie a knot in the end.

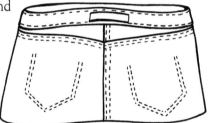

3. Sew the bottom of your jeans together. Starting at one side, push your needle through the front of your jeans to the back, about ½ inch away from the cut edge, and then push it back through to the front to make a stitch about a ¼ inch long.

4. Now, instead of making another stitch forward, push your needle back through your jeans, close to where you started the stitch. Bring the needle back through ¼ inch farther along than the end of your first stitch. This is called a "backstitch" and will make the bottom of your bag strong. Continue to backstitch all the way across the bottom of your jeans.

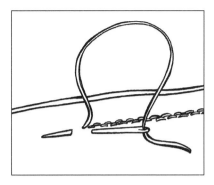

5. Once you have sewn all the way across the bottom, secure your stitches by sewing over the same spot several times. Cut your thread leaving about an inch hanging loose from your final stitch. Turn the bag so that it is right-side out.

GET A HANDLE ON IT

6. Thread the belt through the belt loops of your jeans. Buckle it at the front, just as you would if you were wearing them.

7. Take your scarf and tie one end of it to a belt loop on the left-hand side of your bag and tie the other end around a belt loop on the right-hand side. *Voilà!*

Fabulous tip: Glue on beads, buttons, and sequins using fabric glue to make your bag one-of-a-kind. Why not glue beads onto your bag in the shape of your initials to give it that personal touch?

HOW TO MAKE A FABULOUS FATHER'S DAY GIFT

Great gifts don't have to cost lots of money. Giving somebody your time can mean a lot. Make this fabulous checkbook for your Dad so that he can put his feet up whenever he needs to.

You will need:

five 8 ½ x 11 sheets of plain, white paper • a ruler • a pencil • an eraser • scissors • a black pen • a stapler

1. Take a sheet of paper and, using your ruler and a pencil, draw a rectangle measuring 8 inches by 3 inches. Carefully cut this out.

2. Use this rectangle as a template and trace around it to make four more rectangles. Carefully cut out your rectangles. (Use your other pieces of paper.)

3. Take one of your rectangles and, using your pencil and ruler, design it so that it looks like the rectangle below. This is your check.

To..   Date..................

I promise ....

....

Signed..

4. Trace over the lines you have drawn in black pen and then erase your pencil lines. Repeat this for the other four checks.

5. Now you need to decide what you are going to promise your dad on the checks. Some good ones are: "I promise to make you breakfast in bed," "I promise to wash the car," "I promise not to make any noise while you are watching sports on TV," "I promise to bake you your favorite cake," and "I promise not to be embarrassed when you play air guitar."

6. When your checks are all filled out, put the five sheets in a pile so that they are all facing the same way and staple them together ½ inch in from the left edge.

7. To give your gift, simply place your checkbook inside a card and give it to your dad on Father's Day.

Fabulous tip: Why not make a checkbook for your mom on her birthday or even one for a friend?

HOW TO GIVE YOUR HAIR AN A-MAYO-ZING TREAT

Who knew you could make a moisturizing hair mask from mayo? Open up a jar to unlock the secret to fabulous hair!

You will need:

a wide-toothed comb • 1 small jar of mayonnaise • a disposable shower cap

1. Wash your hair as you would normally, then dry it with a towel.

2. Comb the tangles out of your hair using a wide-toothed comb.

3. Take a handful of mayonnaise and smooth it through your hair, from root to tip, until your hair feels nice and slippery.

4. Comb the mayonnaise through, then put on the shower cap, tucking in all of your hair. Leave it on for half an hour.

5. Take off the shower cap and throw it away. Rinse off all of the mayonnaise. Shampoo your hair again. Dry and style your hair as normal.

Fabulous tip: Wrap a towel around the shower cap during step **4** to allow the heat from your head to intensify the moisturizing power of the hair mask.

HOW TO MAKE A SUMPTUOUS SNOW-WHITE DELIGHT

These white-chocolate wedges are simple to make and utterly delicious. Once your friends and family have tried them, they will beg you to make these fabulous treats again and again.

You will need:

7 oz white chocolate • 7 tablespoons butter
• 4 tablespoons condensed milk • 7 oz shortbread cookies
• 2 tablespoons dried apricots (chopped)
• 2 tablespoons almonds (chopped) • 1 tablespoon raisins
• 1 tablespoon candied cherries • 2 tablespoons of
confectioners' sugar

1. Place a 7-inch, loose-bottomed cake pan on a sheet of parchment paper and draw around it. Carefully cut out the circle. Dip a piece of paper towel into a little butter and rub it around the inside of the pan. Then place the circle of parchment paper in the bottom of the pan.

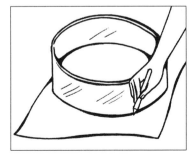

89

2. Break the chocolate into a saucepan, then add the butter and the condensed milk. Melt these ingredients on low heat. Ask an adult to help you with this.

3. When the ingredients are all melted together, remove the pan from the heat and put it aside.

4. Put the cookies in a clear plastic food bag and crush them into crumbs using a rolling pin. Pour the crumbs into the pan.

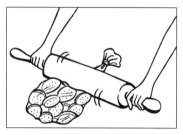

5. Add the cherries, raisins, almonds, and apricots to the pan and stir the mixture.

6. When the mixture is all combined, spoon it into the cake pan. Press and smooth it down with the back of a metal spoon.

7. Put the cake pan in the fridge and let it set overnight.

8. Slide the cake out of the pan and onto a plate. Remove the parchment paper from the bottom and then cut the cake into thick wedges using a butter knife.

Fabulous tip: Sprinkle your white-chocolate wedges with confectioners' sugar to give them a sweet and pretty coating. Serve them with a sprig of fresh mint. Delicious!

HOW TO MAKE A FABULOUS FOAMING BATH POOF

This pretty poof can be either the perfect present for a gal pal or a great way to treat yourself to supersoft skin.

You will need:

3 ft of soft tulle netting in a pretty color (available from your local craft store) • a needle with a large eye • thread in a matching color to the tulle • 1 ½ ft of ribbon • pins

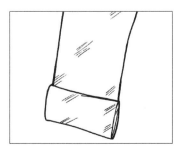

1. Spread the tulle out flat in front of you. Fold it over 4 inches up from the bottom edge. Fold over again and again until all the fabric has been folded into a rectangle that is 4 inches wide.

2. Secure the rectangle of fabric with pins. Sew all the way down the center of the rectangle from one end to the other using a simple backstitch (see page 84). Secure your stitches by sewing repeatedly in the same spot and then tying a knot in your thread.

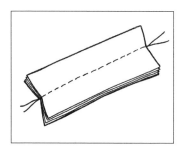

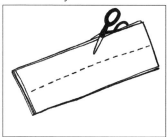

3. Cut carefully along each folded edge of your tulle rectangle, then cut another piece of thread, roughly twice as long as the rectangle. Make a knot in the end of the thread. Using loose stitches, sew along the center of the tulle again.

4. Instead of securing your stitches when you reach the end, remove your needle and pull on the thread, so that the tulle gathers into a pretty poof.

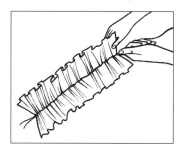

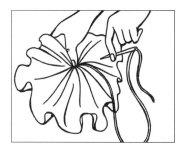

5. Fold the poof into a loop and stitch the ends together. Tie a knot in your thread to secure your stitches. Thread your ribbon through the loop of the poof and tie it into a pretty bow. Fabulous!

HOW TO TWIRL A BATON LIKE A MAJORETTE

Learning to twirl a baton is fantastic fun and a wonderful way to get some exercise. Mastering just one simple move will look really impressive.

LET'S TWIRL, GIRL!

Batons are available from most dance-wear stores, but don't worry if you can't find one right away. Find a stick that is slightly shorter than the length of your arm from shoulder to fingertip. Stick a large lump of modeling clay on each end. Make sure one of your lumps of modeling clay is slightly larger than the other to make the baton heavier at that end.

THE SIDEWAYS FIGURE EIGHT

1. To hold the baton correctly, grip it in the middle with your right hand (if you are right-handed), with your hand on top of the baton. The larger end of your baton (shaded in black) is called the "head," and should point to your left. The smaller end, called the "toe," should point to your right.

2. Unfold your fingers so the baton is resting between your thumb and the palm of your hand. Tilt your hand to your left so that the head of the baton swings downward and your palm is facing forward, as shown.

3. Roll your wrist over so that your palm is facing you and the head of the baton swings upward. Flick the baton with your little finger as you do this to give it some momentum.

4. Now turn your hand and wrist so that your palm faces upward. This will send the baton tumbling away and allow the toe to swing upward toward you.

5. As the head of the baton continues to swing, turn your hand with the movement, so that your palm faces outward and your fingers are pointing to your right.

6. With your palm still facing forward, turn your wrist 180° to your left, swinging the head of the baton downward and back into the starting position. Now repeat steps **2** through **5**.

As you practice, these steps should become one fluid movement that you can repeat without having to stop.

Look at you go!

Fabulous tip: If you are having trouble twirling, follow these steps without the baton in your hand. As your hand goes through the stages, try to imagine you are drawing a sideways figure eight with your fingertips in one smooth motion. When you feel you have got the hang of it, pick up your baton and give it a twirl.

HOW TO GIVE YOUR FACE A WORKOUT

A full facial workout will firm up the muscles in your face and leave it looking and feeling great. Take some time to tone up.

Before you start, rub lots of moisturizer into your face and neck so that your skin feels nice and soft.

CHIN-UPS

Tilt your head back so that your nose is pointing at the ceiling. Press your tongue against the roof of your mouth, and then open your mouth and slowly close it again. You should feel a stretch along your neck and up under your chin. Repeat this ten times, and then slowly lower your head.

BAREFACED CHEEKS

Put your elbows on a table and lean your head into your hands, so that your cheeks are resting against your palms. Let your hands take the weight of your head, so you can feel your cheeks pushing up and outward. Smile as widely as you can, so you can feel your cheeks moving against your hands, then relax. Repeat this ten times.

THE EYES HAVE IT

Raise your eyebrows as high as you can and open your eyes wide. Then close your eyes while keeping your eyebrows raised. Repeat this ten times.

HOW TO MAKE A FABULOUS CAKE STAND

Brighten up your party table with this gorgeous, easy-to-make cake stand. Pile it high with the most superb sweet or savory snacks, for the prettiest way to present your party food.

You will need:

3 pretty party cups (paper or plastic)
• a sharp pencil
• a blob of modeling clay
• 10 ft of curling ribbon • scissors
• 2 small, pretty party plates
• 1 large, pretty party plate
• adhesive tape

1. Place one of your cups on top of a ball of modeling clay. Make a hole in the bottom of the cup by pushing a sharp pencil through the center into the clay. Repeat this with the other cups and the three plates.

2. Fold the ribbon in half and cut it into two equal lengths. Hold the pieces of ribbon together and thread them through the hole in one of the cups. Pull them through.

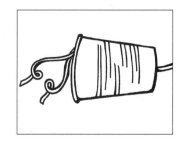

3. Thread the ribbons through the other cups and plates in the following order: through the top of a small plate, through the bottom of the second cup, through the top of the other small plate, and then through the bottom of the last cup.

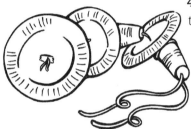

4. Finally, thread the ribbons through the top of the large plate. Secure the ends of the ribbon to the bottom of the final plate with adhesive tape—so they can't slip back through.

5. Take hold of the loose ends of the ribbon on the first cup and sit the cake stand on its base. Bring the cake stand together by pulling on the ribbons and tying the two ends in a knot and then in a pretty bow.

6. Curl the ends of the ribbon by holding them flat against the blade of your scissors at the base of your bow. Carefully scrape the scissors down the length of the ribbon. Let the curls cascade down the tiers of the stand, then load it with your favorite cupcakes.

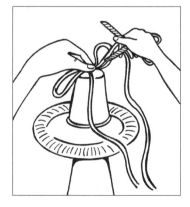

HOW TO TEACH AN OLD COAT NEW TRICKS

Nothing makes winter months seem longer than wearing the same old coat year after year. Why not cheer up dull days by adding some bright buttons and a cute "corsage"—a small bouquet of flowers—to your coat?

BRIGHT BUTTONS

Buttons can be bought very cheaply from craft stores, but if you ask around, you may find someone who has a button box you can raid. It doesn't matter if the buttons don't match one another—just choose a selection you like that are roughly the same size as your coat's existing buttons.

Warning: Check with an adult before cutting the buttons off your coat. They might not think it is a fabulous idea.

You will need:

a selection of buttons • sewing thread
• a needle • scissors • a toothpick

1. Carefully cut the old buttons off your coat using scissors. Remove any thread left behind.

2. Thread your needle. Pull it down to the middle of the thread and then make a double knot to tie the two ends together.

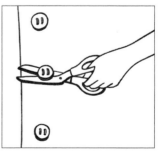

3. Place one of your new buttons over the spot where one of your old buttons used to be.

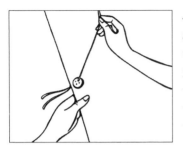

4. Take your threaded needle and push it through from underneath the fabric, straight into one of the buttonholes. Pull the thread all the way through until the knot is anchored underneath.

5. Place your toothpick on top of your button between the holes. Pass the thread over the toothpick and push the needle through the hole opposite and through your coat, until it comes out of the other side.

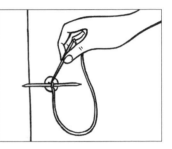

6. Pull the thread taut, and then pass the needle through the first hole again, then back through the hole on the other side. Continue sewing through the button and over the toothpick, until you have done 15 or so stitches. Take the needle back to the inside of the coat.

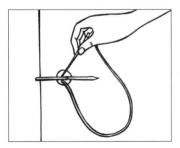

7. If your button is the kind with four holes, start on the other two holes using the method described in steps **5** and **6**. If your button only has two holes, go straight to step **8**.

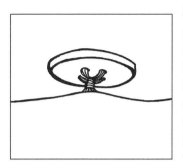

8. When the button feels secure, push the needle to the front of the fabric just beside the button. Remove the toothpick and lift up the button, pulling the threads connecting it to the coat taut. Wrap the thread around the connecting threads 20 times. Then push your needle through to the back of the fabric.

9. Cut your thread, leaving enough length to tie in a double knot. This will hold your button in place.

A CUTE CORSAGE

You will need:

old silk flowers
• a pipe cleaner • a safety pin

1. Trim the stems of the silk flowers until they are just 2 inches long.

2. Arrange the flowers together in a small bouquet. Tie them together by wrapping the pipe cleaner firmly around the stems.

3. Secure the corsage to the lapel of your coat using a safety pin. *Voilà!*

HOW TO BE A FABULOUS GARDENER

Getting your hands dirty might not sound fabulous, but gardening is fun and growing leafy herbs can turn ordinary meals into taste sensations. Don't worry, your fingers won't actually turn green!

You will need:

2 small flowerpots • a packet of mint seeds
• a packet of basil seeds • potting soil • scissors • water

MINT–FRESH AND TASTY

Mint is incredibly easy to grow and is very refreshing when added to summer drinks or leafy salads. Plant the seeds in spring.

1. Fill a pot with soil to 1 inch below the rim.

2. Open your seed packet carefully using a pair of scissors and pour the seeds into the palm of your hand.

3. Sprinkle a small pinch of seeds onto the surface of your soil. Cover them with a very thin layer of soil. Put the rest of the seeds back in the packet.

4. Water your seeds until the soil is wet but not soaked, and leave your pot in a sunny spot such as on a windowsill.

5. Check your pot every day to make sure that the soil is still damp. If it feels a little dry, water it. Your seeds should sprout between 10 and 14 days after planting.

6. Once you have lots of little seedlings growing in the pot, pull out the weakest-looking ones to leave just five strong seedlings.

7. Keep watering your little plants, and in just a few weeks you will be able to eat their delicious leaves. Use scissors to cut leaves from the top of the plant, allowing it to grow bushy at the base.

BASIL—MAKE WAY FOR THE KING OF HERBS

Basil is a yummy herb that is great in pasta sauces and salads (see page 60). Plant in early spring.

1. Plant your basil seeds the same way you planted your mint, but this time cover them with ¼ inch of soil.

2. Basil should sprout in seven to ten days. When your seedlings are big enough for you to handle, pull out all of the weakest-looking ones to leave just three.

3. Your plants will be ready to harvest in six weeks. Simply pinch off the leaves from the top of the plant and enjoy.

Fabulous tip: Make sure you trim off any flowers when they appear so your plants can put all of their energy into producing more delicious leaves.

HOW TO MAKE A TIARA FIT FOR A PRINCESS

This easy-to-make tiara is perfect for parties, or if you like looking utterly fabulous just for the fun of it!

You will need:

2 pipe cleaners 1 ft long
• lots of beads with holes wide enough
to fit over two pipe cleaners

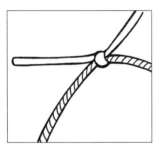

1. Take the two pipe cleaners and connect them by pushing one end of each through a single bead. Push the bead along the pipe cleaners until it is about 2 inches away from the ends.

2. Thread more beads onto the longer end of one of your pipe cleaners, until you have a beaded branch about 2 ½ inches long. This will form the bottom strand of your tiara. Thread more beads on the other pipe cleaner, this time adding a couple extra to make this branch slightly longer than the first. This branch will form the top of your tiara.

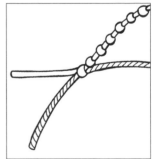

3. Bend the top pipe cleaner over into an arch shape. Bring the two pipe cleaners together by sliding a bead over both ends and pushing it along until it meets the bottom of the beaded branches, forming a loop.

4. Repeat step **2**, this time making two branches about 3 inches long. Add a couple more beads to the top branch like you did before. Bring the pipe cleaners together with a bead to make another loop.

5. Repeat steps **2** and **3** again to form another 2 ½ inch loop, just like the first one you made.

6. Bring both pipe cleaners together and thread more beads over both so they form one strand. Keep threading with beads until you reach ½ inch before the ends. Repeat this for the other two loose ends. Secure your final beads by folding over the ends of the pipe cleaners.

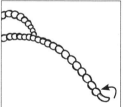

7. Shape your tiara by bending it into the arch shape of a headband. Tweak the loops so that they stand up.

Perfect. Now simply place the tiara on top of your head and find the nearest ball or party to attend.

HOW TO STYLE OUT BEING SHY

You are at a party, in a room full of people you don't know very well, and they all seem to be talking and laughing together. You want to turn around and run—but stop right there! Everybody feels shy sometimes, but if you leave now you could miss out on a really fun time. Follow these tips to help you style out your shyness so you can shine in every situation.

FIVE FABULOUS TIPS

1. When you start to feel nervous, take a few long deep breaths and take a look around. Controlling your breathing will help you feel calmer.

2. Stand up straight with your shoulders back and your arms by your side. This will make you look and feel more confident. Try not to cross your arms or fidget—this can make you look nervous or even moody.

3. Smile—even if you don't feel like it. This will show people that you are happy to be there and that you are a fun person to be around. Not smiling, or even frowning, can make you look bored or rude. This will stop people from coming over to speak to you.

4. Talk to someone. This might seem impossible, but the only way to overcome your fears is to face them. Scan the room for someone who looks as shy as you feel. Making her feel at ease will make you feel more confident. You may even make a new friend! Follow the tips on page 123 to help you out.

5. Take part in party games. This will help pass the time and will give you something to talk to people about when the games are finished. You might find yourself forgetting your shyness and having a good time.

HOW TO MAKE A SPLASH IN DESIGNER RAIN BOOTS

Now you can make a splash in style with a fabulous pair of designer rain boots. You can be sure no one will have a pair quite like yours!

You will need:

a pair of plain rain boots
• a bowl of hot soapy water
• a piece of paper • a pencil
• a felt-tip pen • acrylic paints
• a paintbrush

1. Before you get started, make sure your rain boots are completely clean. Wash them in a bowl of hot, soapy water, then rinse them with clean water and let them dry.

2. Take a piece of paper and a pencil and sketch a design for your rain boots. Choose simple shapes that you can repeat—rainbows or raindrops will look great, or some flashy lightning bolts. Alternatively, you could attempt to brighten up a dull day by drawing colorful summer flowers.

3. When you are happy with your design and your rain boots are completely dry, use your felt-tip pen to draw your design onto your boots. Don't worry if you make a mistake—you can always paint over it later.

4. Fill in the outlines of the shapes using acrylic paints. Choose bright colors to make your design stand out. Let your boots dry.

Now all you need to do is wait for the rain to start falling . . . then jump into the biggest puddle you can find!

Fabulous tip: Acrylic paints are waterproof so your designs will stay bright no matter how muddy the puddles. If the paint begins to chip or flake, though, wash your boots again and touch up your design with a fresh coat of paint.

HOW TO GET VIP TREATMENT FOR FREE

Rich, famous, and fabulous people always get things for free even though they can afford to buy things! Well, now that you are fabulous, the same applies to you.

THE SWEET SMELL OF SUCCESS

Department store beauty counters are usually happy to give away free samples of perfumes and skin treatments (as long as you ask politely and don't go back every week for more). Find the courage to ask. After all, you're not doing anything wrong, and you are a future customer. Save your sweet-smelling samples and skin creams to wear on special occasions. If you are feeling extra brave, you could even ask a salesperson to give you a free makeover.

A TASTE OF THE HIGH LIFE

Believe it or not, the supermarket is a great place for freebies, too. The deli counter often has a selection of tasty treats for hungry shoppers to try. If you don't see anything on the counter, hang around for a while. The sales assistants are sure to offer you something if you are polite when they ask if you need any help.

The same goes for the ice-cream parlor. Before you order, have a good look at all the flavors available. Ask if you can try any of the unusual ones first. Lots of ice-cream parlors encourage this since they want you to buy more ice cream.

Warning: Don't try this if the stores are extra busy. The salespeople are far less likely to help you then, and you could annoy other customers.

HAPPY BIRTHDAY TO YOU ...

Letting a restaurant know that it is either your birthday, or that of one of your friends, is guaranteed to get you the star treatment when you are out for dinner. Tell one of the waiters whose special day it is and wait to see what happens.

Warning: Telling someone it is your birthday can be embarrassing, because it may mean you will have to stand on your chair while the whole restaurant sings to you. Decide whether you think this is worth a free piece of cake.

FIVE FABULOUS WAYS TO WEAR A HEAD SCARF

A head scarf is the perfect accessory for adding a touch of glamour to any outfit. And it's practical, too.

THE HOLLYWOOD HAIR-TAMER

This style is perfect for anyone going for a spin in a cool convertible, or for keeping your hair in place on a windy day.

1. Fold a large, silky scarf in half diagonally to make a triangle.

2. Place the scarf on your head so that the folded edge is even with your hairline and the open side hangs down the back of your head.

3. Carefully cross the corners of the folded edge under your chin and pass them around your neck to the back.

4. Tie the scarf at the nape of your neck, catching the back of the scarf under the knot. Leave the ends of your knot loose or tuck them under for neatness.

Fabulous tip: Pair your head scarf with an enormous pair of sunglasses to increase the celeb factor.

THE BOHO BELT

This belt is perfect in a pant-related emergency, or just to add a splash of color to a summer dress.

1. Fold your scarf in half lengthwise and then in half again to make a long rectangle shape.

2. If you are wearing a dress, simply wrap the scarf around your waist and tie it in a knot at the side. Let the ends hang down.

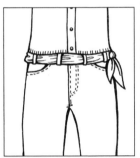

3. If you are wearing pants, feed one end of your folded scarf through the belt loops and tie it in a knot at your hip.

Fabulous tip: Keep adding to your collection of scarves so that you have one to go with every outfit in your wardrobe.

THE NECKERCHIEF

Add fabulous fifties flare to any outfit with this nifty neckerchief.

1. Fold the scarf diagonally to make a triangle.

2. Hold the folded edge to the nape of your neck and then bring the ends to the front, tying it in a knot at the side–simple!

THE GYPSY WRAP

This look is perfect for covering up a bad hair day, or for protecting your hair from the sun.

1. Fold a large, silky scarf in half diagonally to form a triangle.

2. Lay the folded edge 1 inch below your hairline.

3. Pull the corners of the scarf to the back of your head. Tie in a loose knot at the nape of your neck, catching the back of the scarf under the knot.

THE FASHIONISTA HEADBAND

Here's a fabulous way to keep your hair out of your face—and it looks equally good with short or long hairstyles. If you have long hair, put your hair up in a ponytail before you start. This will make tying the scarf much easier.

1. Fold your scarf in half lengthwise and then fold it in half again.

2. Place the scarf on or just behind your hairline and pass it down the sides of your head behind your ears. Tie it tightly at the back of your neck, under your hair, with a double knot to keep it in place. Leave the ends flowing loosely over one shoulder.

3. If you had put your hair in a ponytail, undo it and you're ready to go.

HOW TO HAVE A FABULOUS FLIGHT

Begin and end your vacation in style by following these tips for looking "plane" perfect when you are jetting off.

BEFORE TAKEOFF

• Wear loose-fitting clothes, with layers on your top half. The temperature onboard a flight can go up and down. This way you can keep as cool or as warm as you need.

• Pack a clean top in your carry-on. Turbulence and bad weather can make eating and drinking tricky, and arriving at your destination in dirty clothes is a definite no-no.

• Put long hair back in a neat braid to keep it out of your face. Avoid ponytails as these can make leaning back in your seat uncomfortable.

IN FLIGHT

Sitting still for a long time can cause fluid to build up in your legs and ankles, which makes them swell. To prevent this, get up and move around the cabin as much as you can. When this isn't possible, try these simple exercises in your seat:

Ankle circles. Remove your shoes and imagine you are trying to draw a circle with your big toe. Circle your ankle clockwise and then counter-clockwise. Repeat this ten times with each leg.

Knee lifts. Lift your right knee to your chest and then let it drop. Lift your left knee and let it drop. Repeat this ten times.

Pack a tiny container of moisturizer or aloe and lip balm in your carry-on. Flying can dry out your skin. Apply lip balm and moisturizer at least once every two hours–this will help keep your skin from drying out.

To stop you from feeling high and dry, make sure you drink plenty of water. Avoid sodas–these can dry you out even more.

HOW TO MAKE A FABULOUS FROZEN-YOGURT SHAKE

This frosty fruit shake makes a yummy *brrr*-eakfast and is a great way to start the day.

You will need:
1 ripe banana • 1 small container of yogurt • 10 strawberries

1. Pour the yogurt into each square of your ice-cube tray and then place it in the freezer overnight.

2. In the morning, remove the tray from the freezer and let it stand for 30 minutes. Meanwhile, carefully chop your banana and strawberries into chunks.

3. Pop your yogurty cubes out of the ice-cube tray and put them in the blender. Add the strawberry and banana chunks, then blend it all together for 30 seconds. Pour your shake into a glass and enjoy!

HOW TO MAKE
A MAGICAL MIRROR

"Mirror, mirror, on the wall, who is the fairest of them all?" Well you are—obviously. But could that mirror do with some sprucing up? Follow these simple steps to make your mirror magical.

You will need:

an old mirror with a wooden frame • newspaper
• a sheet of sandpaper • paintbrushes • wood primer
• white emulsion paint • white glue • a clean cloth
• a pile of pretty pictures cut from magazines or gift wrap

1. Protect the surface you are working on with newspaper. Take your sandpaper and rub the frame of the mirror firmly so that some of the wood comes away as dust. Sand around the whole frame until it all looks rough, then wipe away the dust with a damp cloth.

2. Take your paintbrush and give your mirror a coat of wood primer, following the directions on the can. Ask an adult to help you with this. (Be very careful not to get any primer on the glass. If you do, wipe it away quickly with a damp cloth.) When the whole frame is covered, let it dry.

116

3. Paint your frame again, this time with a coat of white emulsion paint, and then let it dry.

4. When your frame is completely dry, it is time to arrange your pictures or gift wrap on the frame. You may just want to put a few pictures in each corner of the frame. Alternatively, for a bolder look, cover the whole frame so there are no white spaces. When you are happy with the position of your pictures, glue them to the frame one at a time. Let your frame dry.

5. Take a clean paintbrush and apply a coat of white glue to your decorated frame. This will give it a shiny, professional finish. Be very careful not to get any glue onto the glass of the mirror. If you do, wipe it off right away.

6. Hang your mirror up on your wall and take a peek.

Now you have a mirror that is as beautiful as you are!

HOW TO SURVIVE A FASHION FIASCO

Imagine you are going to a party. You have put on your favorite new sparkly top and skirt, and you are looking fabulous. But when you arrive at the party, disaster strikes—a girl in your class is wearing the same outfit as you ... exactly the same. What do you do?

HAVE A SENSE OF HUMOR

Go over to your classmate and tell her what wonderful taste she has. She will hopefully see the funny side of this fashion fiasco, and you can have a good giggle about it together.

HOW TO STOP IT FROM HAPPENING AGAIN

• Always wear a new item of clothing as soon as you have bought it. This way it's more likely you'll be the first to be seen in it.

• Always arrive on time to parties. If you get there first, you won't be the copycat when someone arrives later wearing the same thing.

• Make your style your own by customizing old clothes rather than wearing new ones. Glue sequins and beads to old T-shirts using fabric glue, or dress up plain outfits with fabulous accessories such as the handbag on page 84 to rock your own unique style.

HOW TO DINE IN A FANCY RESTAURANT

Having good table manners shows the people you are dining with that you have respect for them and want them to be comfortable eating with you. Gobbling your food or talking with your mouth full are complete no-nos. Follow these tips to become a fabulous dining companion.

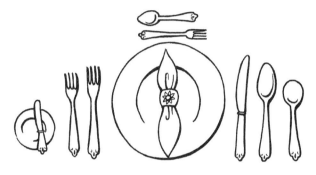

USE A NAPKIN

When you have been seated at your table, remove the napkin from your place setting, unfold it, and put it in your lap. If you leave the table at any point, fold your napkin loosely and put it on the table. Your napkin should only be used for keeping food off your clothes or for dabbing around your mouth. Never use it to blow your nose!

KNIVES AND FORKS

If you have more than one knife and fork in front of you, do not worry. These are for the different courses of food. As a general rule, it is best to start with the cutlery farthest from your plate and then work your way in. The fork and spoon above your plate should be used with dessert.

ROLL WITH IT

Your bread plate will be to the left of your fork. When eating bread, break off one small, bite-sized piece at a time and butter

it just before you eat it. Do not butter a big piece and then take a bite. It is much nicer to be ready to contribute to a conversation without having to put a piece of half-eaten bread back on your plate.

THE GOLDEN RULES OF FINE DINING

• **Do** ask politely for people to pass things to you, rather than reaching across their plates.

• **Do** remember to say "Please" and "Thank you" to the people who are serving you.

• **Do** wait for everyone to be served before you start eating, unless you are told otherwise.

• **Don't** say that something is gross or that you do not like your meal unless there is something very wrong with it.

• **Do** ask permission before you leave the table to go to the bathroom.

• **Do** put your knife and fork side-by-side on your plate when you have finished eating. This tells the waiters that it can be taken away.

• **Do** thank the people who invited you to dinner and tell them what you enjoyed the most.

HOW TO GIVE YOURSELF A PROFESSIONAL PEDICURE

Walking, running, and even standing still all put your feet under pressure. Make your feet fabulous with this ultimate pampering pedicure.

You will need:

a basin filled with water • towels
• a capful of bubble bath • cotton balls
• nail-polish remover • a pumice stone
• a pair of nail clippers • a nail file • moisturizing cream
• tissues • nail polish

1. First remove any old nail polish. Soak a cotton ball in nail-polish remover and rub this over your nails until they are polish free. Never pick off old polish because this can damage the surface of your nails.

2. Lay a towel on the floor in front of a comfortable chair and half fill a basin with warm water and some bubble bath. Carry the basin carefully and lay it on the towel. Take a seat and soak your feet in the basin for ten minutes. Then pat your feet dry with a towel.

3. Take your nail clippers and cut your toenails straight across the tips.

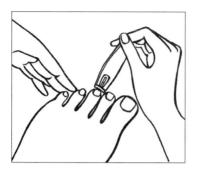

Don't try to cut them in one snip but gently take off bits of nail with the clippers. Always leave an area of white at the top of the nail. This will ensure you haven't cut them too short.

4. Clean up your trimmed toenails using a nail file. Gently sweep the flat edge of the file across the tops of your nails to smooth down any rough edges. Again, don't try to shape your nails, but keep the tips straight.

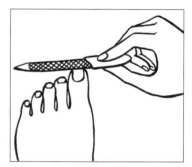

5. Take a look at your soaked feet. If patches of skin on your heels feel rough and you can scrape some off with your fingernail, this is dead skin. Remove it by rubbing with the rough pumice stone. Don't rub too hard since young feet don't have much hard, dead skin on them.

6. Once you're happy that your feet feel baby soft, rinse them with clean water.

7. Dry your feet well with the towel and apply a generous amount of moisturizer or, if you have some, foot cream. Let this soak in while you choose a nail polish color.

8. Before you start painting your nails, separate your toes with a folded tissue. Take the tissue and fold it over and over again lengthwise until you have a band about ¾ inch wide. Thread it between your toes. This will keep your toes from moving and messing up your polish.

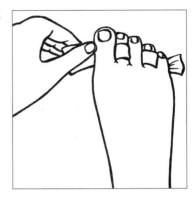

9. Wipe the surface of your nails with a tissue to remove any moisturizer. Take your nail polish and do the first coat. Let it dry before applying a second coat. Wait at least 30 minutes before putting on your most fabulous flip-flops.

HOW TO BE FABULOUS AT TALKING TO PEOPLE

Starting up conversations with new people can be tricky and make you feel shy. Follow these tips to make sure that you are never at a loss for words.

DOS AND DON'TS

• **Do** remember that conversations are a two-way thing. Share your opinions, but also ask the other person questions about what he or she thinks.

• **Do** pay attention and really listen to what people are saying. This shows that you find them interesting.

• **Do** use someone's name when addressing him or her.

• **Do** make eye contact to show that you are paying attention to that person and not looking for someone else to talk to.

• **Do** start questions with "What," "Where," "Which," or "Who," since these require longer answers and start up a good conversation. Avoid starting questions with "Are you" or "Do you," because you might just get a yes or no answer.

• **Don't** interrupt. It can make people lose the thread of what they were saying or make them think that they are boring.

THE "FORE" FABULOUS RULES

There are some things that everyone has in common. Try and memorize these "FORE" rules for fabulous conversations.

Family—everyone comes from somewhere. Ask them if they have any brothers and sisters and whether they are older or younger.

Occupation—everyone fills their days with something. Ask them where they were before coming to this event or what they would normally be doing if they weren't here.

Recreation—everyone likes to do something in their spare time, whether it's watching their favorite show on television or skydiving. Asking what people do in their spare time will get them talking about the things they love most.

Education—everyone you are likely to meet has either been or goes to school. Ask them which school they go to or went to and what their favorite subject is or was.

HOW TO WALK YOUR DOG WITH STYLE

Getting out into the great outdoors should never be a chore. Going on a brisk walk is fabulous exercise and will brighten your skin. Don't worry if you don't have a dog–follow these tips to look your best on a walk in the park or a day out in the country.

LOOKING THE PART

Style is important, but wearing your favorite party shoes, no matter how fabulous they are, is not recommended. You might look a bit silly, and you could end up ruining them. So, before you leave the house, choose from these three fabulous looks:

Country lady: Tuck your jeans into your rain boots and put on a hat or a headscarf to protect your hair from the wind.

Sporty sister: Put on a clean pair of sweatpants, a stylish T-shirt, and some sneakers. Complete your look with a cool baseball cap.

Urban cool: Pair your favorite pair of jeans with a pair of comfortable walking shoes and a vest. Complete the look with a snazzy to-go mug and a magazine.

HOW TO AVOID THE PAPARAZZI

Being as fabulous as you are is, well, fabulous. But it can have its drawbacks. People are going to want to follow your every move. You may even start to attract the attention of local photographers who will want to photograph you every time you leave the house. Follow these tips to keep yourself out of the gossip magazines.

DAMSEL IN DISGUISE

• **Do** carry a head scarf and an enormous pair of sunglasses wherever you go. These can make a great disguise. See pages 111 to 113 for tips on how to tie your scarf.

• **Do** carry a newspaper or magazine. You can hold this over your face if flashes start going off.

• **Do** buy a wig. Cheap ones are available at party stores and will change your appearance dramatically.

MADEMOISELLE OF MYSTERY

• **Don't** always tell everyone your plans for the weekend. You never know who might leak the information to the press. Make sure you tell your parents, though. Besides, you may need them to help you make a quick getaway.

• **Do** arrive and leave an event through the back door. This will throw photographers off your trail.

• **Do** beat the paparazzi at their own game. Carry a camera and if they start taking pictures of you, take pictures of them right back. They won't like it.

FOLLOW THE GOLDEN RULES OF STARDOM

1. Always make sure you look your best before leaving the house. An extra five minutes at the mirror could spare you the embarrassment of receiving an award for "Worst Hairdo of the Year."

2. Always make sure you are as fabulous as you can be to everyone you meet. This will make them your future fans, and it may stop them from selling mean stories about you.

3. Always make sure you stop to sign autographs when you aren't in too much of a hurry (see page 47).

4. Never be rude to the paparazzi. If you are, they might choose to print the worst pictures they take of you.